preparing
for

CHANGE
REACTION

preparing
for

CHANGE
REACTION

how to introduce change
in your church

BOB WHITESEL

wesleyan
publishing
house

Indianapolis, Indiana

Copyright © 2007 by Wesleyan Publishing House
Published by Wesleyan Publishing House
Indianapolis, Indiana 46250
Printed in the United States of America
ISBN: 978-0-89827-364-9

Library of Congress Cataloging-in-Publication Data

Whitesel, Bob.
  Preparing for change reaction : how to introduce change to your church
/ Bob Whitesel.
      p. cm.
  Includes bibliographical references.
  ISBN 978-0-89827-364-9
  1. Church renewal. I. Title.
  BV600.3.W53 2007
  253—dc22

                                    2007034310

To my wonderful wife of thirty-three years, Rebecca;
our daughters and sons-in-law, Breanna, Mark, Kelly, Corrie, Dave,
and Ashley; and our granddaughter, Cate.

About the Cover
The cover art was chosen to symbolize the dilemma in which the local church often finds herself, where a once vibrant and mobile organization (symbolized by the recreational vehicle on the cover) finds herself exhausted, depleted and immobile—lost in a wilderness of cultural change. The impending storm clouds further emphasize this uncertainty. Yet with clear Biblical understanding of change, the church can become mobile and dynamic again. It is toward this end that this book is aimed.

CONTENTS

HOW TO USE THIS BOOK

CHURCH LEADERS

This book will help church leaders introduce change to a church. In addition, it will help those leading change to investigate, discuss, and build consensus about God's view of change. Thus, each chapter concludes with questions for group study that are designed to help leaders work together in discovering God's viewpoint on change and successfully address the change reactions of church members.

To use the questions for group study it may be best to:

1. Have church leaders read one chapter and jot down their responses to the questions before a leadership event or scheduled meeting.
2. Share and discuss the questions from one chapter as your devotional during the meeting.

Since this book is designed to help you grasp a biblical understanding of change, this exercise can be an effective channel for:

- introducing change to a hesitant congregation
- introducing change in a slow, circumspect manner
- building consensus about change before tackling change
- establishing an understanding of which things should change—and which should not—based on the Bible.

STUDENTS

Students, teachers, seminar leaders, denominational leaders and anyone interested in studying the dynamics of change will discover that the more complex issues are addressed in endnotes. By making use of these notes and the additional resources mentioned therein, the academic reader will be led to a deeper investigation of the topic of change.

However, the principal audience for this book remains church leaders, both volunteers and paid staff members, who have an interest in building consensus in their congregations on the topic of change. Thus, the majority of this book will define a basic understanding of biblical change and how to foster this among Christians. Yet the studious reader also will find here a good starting place for launching a deeper investigation into God's perspective on change.

ACKNOWLEDGMENTS

I would like to thank my colleagues at Wesleyan Publishing House for producing this resource to help pastors, volunteer church leaders, students, and denominational leaders implement and understand a biblical theology of change.

In addition, I would like to thank my colleagues at Indiana Wesleyan University, especially Dr. Henry Smith, Dr. Jim Fuller, Dr. Russ Gunsalus and Dr. David Smith, along with Dr. David Wright from Azusa Pacific University, and Dr. Mark Smith from Ohio Wesleyan University, for their encouragement and friendship during my quest to foster more world-changers in our churches. I am also grateful for my peers at Fuller Theological Seminary, where the ideas contained within this book emerged amid my Ph.D. research into church change in a postmodern world. Fuller professors Dr. Eddie Gibbs, Dr. Ryan Bolger, and Dr. Gary McIntosh, along with Dr. Kent Miller at Michigan State University, have been helpful beyond measure in codifying my thoughts and stimulating my investigation. And, my colleagues in church growth consulting: Dr. Kent Hunter, Dr. Chip Arn, Dr. Alan McMahan, Dr. Erich Baumgartner, Dr. Ed Stetzer, and Dan Kimball have been extraordinarily supportive and insightful. In addition, my students at Indiana Wesleyan University and Fuller Theological Seminary have been helpful in offering their suggestions, insights, and reactions.

I also thank my most important support network: my family. My wife, Rebecca, has been my best friend and prayer partner for over a quarter century, and our daughters, Breanna, Kelly, Corrie, and Ashley, bring sparkle, vivacity, and happiness to my life. Plus, my granddaughter, Cate, brings me a glimpse of the wholesomeness, graciousness, and joy of heaven.

But it is my Lord and Savior Jesus Christ to whom I owe the deepest gratitude. He has redeemed and redirected me, saved me and conscripted me for His service. For His unchanging love, grace, forgiveness, and salvation, I am eternally indebted.

BIOGRAPHICAL NOTE

Dr. Bob Whitesel is associate professor of graduate studies in ministry in the College of Graduate Studies at Indiana Wesleyan University, Marion, Ind. (www.indwes.edu), and president of C3 International (Creative Church Consulting, Intl.; www.c3intl.org). He is a sought-after writer, speaker, consultant, and lecturer on the organic emerging church, church management, and church growth.

Dr. Whitesel's previously published works include:

> *Inside the Organic Church: Learning from 12 Emerging Congregations*
>
> *Growth by Accident, Death by Planning: How Not to Kill a Growing Congregation*
>
> *Staying Power: Why People Leave the Church Over Change and What You Can Do About It*
>
> *A House Divided: Bridging the Generation Gaps in Your Church* (coauthored with Kent R. Hunter)

To communicate with Dr. Bob Whitesel, visit www.bobwhitesel.com or www.TheOrganicChurch.com.

part one

CHURCH CHANGE

change reaction 1

we don't have a plan
for change.

the problem

change has been handled in
so many conflicting and
disorganized ways, that
congregants demand a clear
and simple plan before
accepting change.[1]

change
reactions

Ray was a long-standing leader in his congregation. Well over seventy years of age, Ray's hearing was no longer what it had been, and he gingerly answered my questions in a volume that did not go unnoticed nor unappreciated by fellow leaders nearby. "I've got no problem with change," he declared. "It's the way people want it that bothers me. They want it *now*, and they want *me* to change. I'm tired of it! If they want to do the changin' that's fine, but don't change what the Bible says and don't change me."

Ray presented an irascible demeanor, yet he was a faithful leader in this declining church. "I've been coming here since I was two months old," he recalled. "I've seen good change—and plenty of bad change. Mostly I'm concerned the church is going to die." The volume of his conversation and many nodding heads confirmed that although this church had become wary of change, that concern was overshadowed by a fear that it had failed at initiating effective and appropriate change. As a result this church was dying of *geriatrophy*—congregational old age.[2]

"It's the way you do change," Ray reiterated. "It's not helpful." With that final statement, the after-church lunch concluded, and the pastor convened my informal meeting with about three dozen congregants from this declining church. Once a sizeable, influential congregation, attendance now hovered around fifty in a sanctuary that seated nearly four hundred. Every Sunday, the miniscule attendance in a cavernous sanctuary reminded attendees that the church was on the verge of collapse and that attempts at change had been mismanaged or insufficient.

"We are considering Dr. Whitesel as our consultant," said the pastor. "He is here to help us tackle the things we need to do to reach young people like him." *Young people* in his vernacular meant baby boomers (that generation born between 1946 and 1964) as well as Generations X and Y (those born in or after 1963).[3] The gathering that day comprised mostly congregants aged sixty-five and above; and though a baby boomer myself, I appreciated being lumped in with the "young people."

An analysis of this congregation's history revealed that it had often initiated change to reach younger generations. In each circumstance polarization and suspicion had resulted from the change process, so the church eventually pulled back from implementing change. Subsequently, change proponents went elsewhere. The result was that bad experiences with change had led the leaders to withdraw to familiar strategies and ministries. The consequence was that change was disturbing, intimidating, alarming, and ignored—at least until the impending death of this congregation forced its leaders to attempt one last journey into the mysterious, unfamiliar realm of change.

As I continued to delve into the history (a requisite endeavor for anyone who wants to help a church strategically plot its future), I found this church modeled many of the change reactions I typically find in congregations leery of change.

CHANGE REACTION STRATEGIES

For effective change to take place, two major efforts are needed. The first is to listen for change reactions and to address each appropriately. This allows congregants to be heard and to know leaders are considering their concerns. It also increases communication between those pushing for change (change proponents) and those who are reticent about change (defenders of the status quo). This is strategy A.

The second effort, strategy B, is to establish *change boundaries*. In chapter 7, I will propose a simple eight-step process to discover what values, standards, principles, and traits are important in each church—those things congregants deem beyond changing. Often those reticent about change do not fear the process but rather the outcome of change. They fear change will go too far. Thus, establishing boundaries for change alleviates anxiety, resistance, and antagonism.

If conducted vigilantly, prudently, and concurrently, strategies A and B will bring about effective and unifying change.

Let's learn more about each strategy.

Strategy A: Listen to and Address Change Reactions

Most change attempts are thwarted early in the process. In another book I described the six stages of change and demonstrated that unless input from all congregants, even reticent members, is solicited, change usually fails.[4] The key is to solicit and hear people's concerns, worries, and input before any change is initiated.

Listening for change reactions and carefully addressing as many as feasible will help bring consensus and unity. Research demonstrates that unifying change is more likely to occur if this is done first.[5] Therefore, this book is structured around ten common reactions to change.

Strategy B: Create Change Boundaries

Listening to and answering change reactions is not enough to alleviate the fear of change and bring unity. Reticent congregants must be assured change will not cross certain boundaries. Wary congregants must know there are theological, moral, and congregational limits to proposed change. This book will help you and your church define those boundaries, both theological and practical, within your congregation.

In chapter 7 we will discover eight steps that enable church leaders to design and promote a team-based Statement of Change Boundaries (SCB). This SCB will ensure that change does not go too far, too soon. And, this statement will alleviate concern among reticent congregants that change might take them or the church in a direction they are unwilling to go.

The success of church change depends upon addressing change reactions (strategy A) by producing a mutually accepted SCB (strategy B).

TEN CHANGE REACTIONS

Here are the ten change reactions that will frame our discussion. They are not the only possible reactions and may not be the most prevalent. Yet these reactions and the responses to them form an outline for discovering a biblical understanding of how churches can change in methodology without changing in theology or character.

1. We don't have a plan for change.
2. Our leaders are not good at bringing about change.
3. Do we really need to change?
4. If God doesn't change, why should we?
5. What does the Bible say about change?
6. Let's not talk about change; I need a break.
7. What are we going to change, and what's going to stay the same?
8. You're trying to change things too fast!
9. We've tried change and failed. We'll never be able to do it.
10. What are you doing to help us change, Pastor?

> **change reaction 1** we don't have a plan for change.
> change has been handled in so many conflicting and disorganized ways,
> congregants want a clear and simple plan to bring about change.

This is a common change reaction, for most churches do not have a plan for change—only an idea and a will. While it is necessary to have a vision for change and a will to accomplish it, the change process often stalls because there is not a clear, straightforward *plan* for change. You'll find the help you need for developing a plan in chapters 3–9.

This book will answer these and other questions:

- If God is unchangeable, why does He sometimes change (a biblical theology of change)?
- What are the eight types of biblical change, and why does God change in two of the types?
- Why does successful change require strategic, tactical, *and* operational leaders?
- How can the pattern of parenting help churches manage change?
- Why do churches spit over change (and how do we prevent that outcome)?
- Why must we go slowly to succeed?

- How can a church create an SCB to ensure that change will not go too far or too fast?

> **change reaction 2** our leaders are not good at bringing about change.
> congregations are cynical about church change, often because change
> is undertaken in a disuniting and ineffective manner.

At the onset of conversations with leaders like Ray, I often find an initial wariness and even hostility toward change. However, after deeper conversation I usually discover congregants are not wholly against change but rather the manner in which it has been handled.

Most of the congregations I advise have attempted change with inconclusive and/or dissatisfying results. Often the pastor and/or church leaders have some idea of a change that is needed, but there is a missing link between the leader's vision and the step-by-step plan the loyal church worker needs. I will show in chapter 2 that the missing link is *tactical leaders* who can organize, plan, budget, recruit volunteers, and evaluate progress of change.

These tactical leaders are the critical go-betweens between visionary strategic leaders and frontline church workers. If they are not in place, the management of the change process will be muddled and mishandled and usually fail. Then, congregants become cynical. A mishandling of change in the church's past may be so painful that the church avoids change at all cost until its survival is in question.

Thus, chapter 2 will discuss how to develop the "tactical leaders" a church needs to plan for change.

> **change reaction 3** do we really need to change?
> some change is needed for a church to stay relevant, thus congregations
> believe some change is warranted—but elusive.

Today we live in a growing mixture of ethnicities, generations, affinity groups, and socio-economic levels. Therefore, within this matrix of people it is no longer sufficient to rely on denominational affiliation to draw people into congregations. Rather, the growing stew pot[6] of subcultures requires churches, much like the apostle Paul, to "become all things to all men so that by all possible means I might save some" (1 Cor. 9:22). This is the attitude of a missionary, and many who are concerned that the church must regain her evangelistic emphasis have described such churches as "missional churches."[7]

If you converse with church leaders at length you'll often find congregants know to reach out to different generations, cultures, or ethnicities they must change their ministry methods much as a missionary would. But congregants are leery about unproductive and ruinous results that have accompanied past change attempts.

The result is that while some change is considered, congregants are wary of change that is not carefully analyzed and then conducted in a professional, unhurried, and logical manner. Congregations understand that change can be productive or destructive—they have experienced it. Thus, because so many painful partings have occurred when change is mismanaged,[8] they want future change to be handled in a circumspect and judicious manner.

Chapter 3 will deal with the critical need for some churches to embrace change in methodology if they are to reach more people for Jesus Christ and make the good news relevant to people today.

change reaction 4 if God doesn't change, why should we?
congregations are leery of church change because
they know God is unchanging in His nature.

Though some change appears to be needed, confusion is often fostered because God's unchangeable nature is emphasized in the Scriptures. Though we shall go into depth on this issue in chapters 4 and 5, a few Scriptures here may be helpful. For instance, God is unlike humans and remains the same (Ps. 102:27), and He is a God "who does not change like shifting shadows" (James 1:17). The result is that most change can be viewed as unbiblical, because it is unclear when church change can undermine or conflict with God's unchanging character.

Chapter 4 will help the reader understand that change must have as its starting place a biblical theology that God is unchanging in His permanence, nature, will, and character.[9]

> **change reaction 5** what does the Bible says about change?
> congregations know some church change has been good, especially when
> it increases a church's effectiveness at sharing the good news.

Further confusion can be fostered when Christians observe that some church change has been helpful and needed. How then is this to be reconciled with the above statements about the unchangeableness of God's character?

Muddying the waters are the positive church changes brought about by reformers such as Martin Luther and John Wesley, or God's changing methodology in His dealings with Israel in the Old and New Testaments. And what about the apostle Paul's statement: "I have become all things to all men so that by all possible means I might save some" (1 Cor. 9:22)?

Chapter 5 will describe a biblical theology of change recognizing that though God never changes in His character, will, nature, or permanence, He does change in the way He deals with us based on our responses to Him. Regarding Paul's statement above, theologian and author George Hunter observes that Paul "does not change the (biblical) message, but (he) changes the style from one context to another."[10] Paul, mirroring his Heavenly Father, does not change in his will or character of compassion, passion, and holiness; but Paul does adjust his methodology, though all the time remaining consistent with godly character, will, and nature.

change reaction 6 let's not talk about change, I need a break.
Leaders are tired of administrative unproductiveness and disorder and want a break from volunteering. After all, isn't church more than administration?

There is further confusion today regarding the church's nature: Is it a spiritual organization or an administrative organization? The great Christian thinker Emil Brunner pointed out that the key to effective church leadership is to recognize that the church is comprised of *two* elements.

The primary element of a church is that it is a *spiritual fellowship* or *supernatural organization* that requires pastoring, consoling, nurturing, and spiritual growth.[11] But, Brunner also points out that the church is an *organizational fellowship* or *administrative organization* that must be managed, administered, and united toward common and biblical goals.[12] Brunner and others have retraced church history to demonstrate that when both of these natures are equally balanced, church growth occurs.[13]

Often the attention and time of church leadership is unbalanced, with either the administrative organization or the spiritual organization taking precedence. But, *organizational leadership* and *spiritual leadership* are inextricability connected, and most church leaders would concur with Brunner that a church flourishes when both are in balance and mutually effective.

Regrettably, if our churches do not balance spiritual leadership with the logical, effective, and strategic management of the organizational fellowship, they can become close-knit communities with dysfunctional leadership systems. In these churches congregants cherish fellowship but avoid volunteering (or grumble when they do), for fellowship is infinitely more enjoyable (and better managed) than its administrative counterpart. In such venues volunteer conscription has been likened to the "wounded buffalo" approach. In this method of recruitment based loosely on Native American hunting lore: Once a buffalo herd scatters, the hunters concentrate on the weak or young buffalos because they are less likely to avoid capture. Similarly, many of our congregations recruit volunteers from a dwindling pool of new and/or loyal congregants who can't avoid conscription. While in such organizations fellowship may be increasingly lauded, volunteerism is increasingly avoided. The result is an increasing bitterness and hopelessness arises among those who continue to volunteer, partnered with a growing guilt among those who drop out of volunteer duties, followed by a mounting disappearance of once-productive church volunteers.

Thus, chapter 6 will investigate how the pattern of parenting can be an effective leadership model for passing the leadership baton to younger generations. We'll see how parents adjust their methodology but not their core beliefs as a child matures. Then we'll look at how congregations can adjust their strategies without compromising their foundational principles and values.

> **change reaction 7** what are we going to change, and what's going to stay the same? congregants want a process to distinguish between when change is warranted and when it is not.

Since congregants know part of God's biblical nature is His unchangeableness, they may have difficulty reconciling God's unchangeableness with needed changes in the church. When this tension is coupled with long-standing traditions older congregants appreciate and want to perpetuate, change is largely seen as a negative experience. As a result, church leaders want to have a judicious process to uncover when change is warranted, and in which areas—such as in theology or methodology—change is not acceptable.

Chapter 7, How to Create Statements of Change Boundaries, provides an eight-step model for identifying areas a local congregation deems unchangeable. The reader will see how a theology of church change can be lived out in an environment where leaders maintain principles while adjusting and changing methodology consistent with their foundational beliefs. A statement that will guide and delineate this process will be called an SCB, and it can help churches communicate how far change will go and boundaries that it will not overstep.

> **change reaction 8** you're trying to change things too fast!
> church leaders sense that effective change should be possible if
> conducted in a slow, but steady and unifying manner.

What might happen if appropriate change were managed in a more unifying and agreeable manner in our churches? What if new attendees from younger generations found amenable and nurturing venues for their new ideas and new strategies? What if a church could distinguish between needed changes and excessive or superfluous ones?

We will look at research that reveals change is doomed if it takes place before broad support and input is achieved. We'll see the six stages of effective change, and discover the most important lesson is to go slowly and attain broad support before moving ahead.

Chapter 8, Go Slowly, Build Consensus, and Succeed, will deal with bringing about change in an atmosphere of slow, steady progress, where appropriate change unifies a congregation.

> **change reaction 9** we've tried change and failed. we'll never be able to do it.
> churches have sincerely tried change, thus the fault may not lie with church leadership
> or congregants. It may be ministerial training that is at fault.

As an educator, I believe the problem lies in part with the education and equipping we provide church leaders in the science of change management. Much of pastoral education revolves around theological, ethical, and historical knowledge, with little emphasis on the administration and management of the church as an organization. As we have seen, Emil Brunner stressed that both the spiritual side as well as the organizational side of a congregation must be addressed for a church to be healthy.[14]

Many in academia seek to right this omission in ministerial education. In the chapter on training for change, the reader will see I believe the study of change must be a central part of our ministerial preparation process if we are to be effective and unifying in our change strategies and processes. If church leaders do not have the option of studying in our schools, a growing cadre of trained, experienced church-growth consultants will be needed to guide the church through the mechanisms of congregational change.

> **change reaction 10** what are you doing to help us change, pastor? the conscientious church leader prepares for change reactions while planning for unifying change and staying connected.

Preparing for change reactions begins with an understanding of change, when it is warranted and when it is not, and then moves on to fostering appropriate change in an effective, unifying manner. Church leaders with even a short tenure will know that change is one of the most misunderstood and divisive topics churches will tackle.

Thus, staying connected during the change process with those you serve cannot be ignored. Churches that try to do so will sense a bubbling cauldron of misery and mystery surging below the surface of the congregational life. Change is the nine-hundred-pound gorilla no one can ignore, but that hasn't stopped church leaders from trying to avoid it.[15]

BOOK OF CHANGE REACTIONS AND CHANGE BOUNDARIES

This book was written to address the change reactions above and to establish SCBs that can foster unchangeable principles amid changing methodologies.

Subsequently, this book will suggest strategies and tools church leaders can use with their boards, denominational leaders can employ with leaders under their oversight, and students in university and graduate level studies can deploy to foster a biblical and effective understanding of appropriate church change—understanding when it is warranted and when it is not.

QUESTIONS FOR GROUP STUDY

Each chapter concludes with questions for group study to help church leaders share insights on change with their boards, committees and fellow leaders. These questions were designed so that

- Church leaders could read one chapter at a time, and discuss the questions at reoccurring meetings.
- Small groups, including Sunday school classes, can discuss the issue of change in a direct, simple, unifying manner.
- Leadership retreats, seminars, courses, and training can become avenues for idea exchange, brainstorming, and dialogue that will help bring many voices into the conversation regarding when and why church changes are appropriate.
- Church leaders can arrive on a biblical and unifying understanding of change, including what should be changed and what should not.

A GREAT COMMISSION FOCUS

Finally, but certainly not least, my purpose is to help churches adopt appropriate change in methodology so more people might hear the good news of Jesus Christ (Matt. 28:19) and encounter Jesus Christ as their personal Savior (John 3:8, 16, 36). It is toward that goal, introducing people to my Lord and Savior Jesus Christ, and not just to tackle the thorny issue of change, that this book is directed.

change reaction 2

our leaders are not good at bringing about change.

the problem

congregations become cynical about change when it is undertaken in a ineffective or disuniting manner.

why is change so difficult to manage?

It happened one Sunday in 1962: my dad stopped going to church. Mother and I still attended, at least for the next year or so. But soon our family no longer frequented the church my parents had attended since they were married.

Dad had been the head usher for the second of three Sunday services in this church of fifteen hundred attendees. In that role he had organized sixteen to twenty men each Sunday to receive the offering and help congregants find seats. Planning was minimal. Dad was supervised by Bill, the church's usher supervisor, who recruited, selected, trained, and mentored ushers. Bill was an engineer for Delco-Remy, where he led a department in the burgeoning lighting division.

However, my father's duties as head usher for the second service were more straightforward. Dad had to ensure that each usher had enough bulletins, that ushers were at all entrances, and on occasion he had to conscript ushers from the audience if someone was missing. This was Dad's close-knit fellowship, and he often remarked that not since his World War II days had he enjoyed such camaraderie.

Dad also prayed over the offering. And because his prayer never changed, I can recall it to this day; Gerald was an operational leader and he liked consistency, uniformity, and reliability. And because he exemplified these traits, he had been head usher of the second service for four years.

Why would a man of such consistency and reliability suddenly disconnect himself from his church? As a child I never understood or inquired. But once grown, I had occasion to ask my dad about his departure. Gerald's disappearance was due to an honor. The faithful discharge of his duties as a head usher had brought him to the attention of the church leaders. When Bill the usher supervisor quit, Gerald was the natural choice to replace him. After all, my dad was head usher for the largest of three services. And he was faithful. Dad was honored, but also wary. Nonetheless after some gentle prodding by the church leaders, Dad was rewarded with a promotion to usher supervisor.

In this new capacity, Dad was thrust into a leadership role that required oversight of sixty-plus men. His duties now included scheduling and organizing ongoing usher training, recruitment, and oversight, as well as replacing ineffective ushers. Dad had enjoyed his duties as head usher of one service, but now his responsibilities doubled, if not tripled. While his previous duties had been largely relational, now his tasks were increasingly organizational. Dad missed the interpersonal nature of his previous duties, and now saw himself increasingly isolated from the fellowship and camaraderie he had previously relished.

Additionally, the usher ministry suffered. Dad found it difficult to schedule pertinent and timely training, and never felt comfortable with the recruitment and dismissal process. Dad was a man everyone liked, and he found it hard not to use a willing usher candidate simply because of lack of skill, decorum, or call.

The church leaders noticed this decline in the usher ministry. They tried to work with Gerald subtly. They tried to develop him into a director who could oversee sixty-plus men and three different worship services. In the end this was not Dad's gifting or calling. Dad had been a sergeant during World War II, and he had successfully led a small team of men. But when it came to the oversight, tactical planning, recruitment, and paperwork necessary to administrate a burgeoning ministry, Dad neither enjoyed it nor felt called to do it.

The church leaders did not want to see Gerald quit, but the atmosphere of pressure and disappointment became too much. Without an avenue for retreat, one day Gerald simply called the church office and resigned. Dad was a gracious and loving man. The eldest child, everyone seemed to like him. But the feelings that he had let down his church and lost his camaraderie were too much. Dad couldn't bear to see the looks of the other ushers, who he felt he had failed as leader, so returning to church was too uncomfortable to bear. Dad simply faded away, and soon our family did as well.

STRATEGIC, TACTICAL, AND OPERATIONAL LEADERSHIP

In adulthood I began investigating leadership styles and always wondered what had happened to my Dad's volunteerism. Dad had been so content and fulfilled as a sergeant in the military. But at church his involvement had led to disappointment and failure. As I researched leadership abilities, I found the military had an insightful understanding of leadership sectors that might benefit the church. It has to do with three military leadership categories: strategic, tactical, and operational.[1]

Strategic Leaders

In History. The word *strategy* comes from the Greek word for a military general: *strategoi.* The generals of ancient Athens, led by the forward-thinking Pericles, undertook a grand building project to make Athens the cultural and political center of Greece. The Athenian generals' strategy paid off with beautiful buildings such as the Parthenon, heralding Athens as the leading Greek city.

Subsequently, in the military field the word *strategic* has come to refer to the bigger-picture planning that is done before a battle begins. Strategic leaders see the big picture and envision outcomes before the battle commences. They intuitively know what the results should be, even though they are not experts in getting there. In the military strategic leaders are generals, admirals, and so forth.

In Architecture. An analogy from the world of art may be helpful. Strategic leaders are akin to artists. They see the dim outline of the future, perhaps a gleaming office tower or an eye-catching museum. They can envision what it will look like once it is complete. But, they see only general forms, shapes, and appearances. They see the art and the results. We will develop this analogy more when we discuss tactical leaders.

In the Military. Strategic leaders are intentional, bigger-picture leaders who deal in theoretical, hypothetical concepts and strategies. For example, in World War II generals such as Dwight Eisenhower and Bernard Montgomery strategically knew France must be invaded and wrested from the German occupiers. The decisions to invade North Africa, Sicily, Italy, and eventually France were decided upon by the generals. But, once each of the invasions commenced, leadership was put into the hands of tactical leaders.

In the Church. Let's look at characteristics that distinguish leaders in the church. Pastors may be drawn into the ministry by two competing roles, the shepherd and the visionary.[2]

Many pastors enter the ministry due to a desire to help humankind with a hands-on, relational, personal, mentoring leadership style. This is analogous to the guidance of a shepherd and is reflected in Scriptures about nurture, care and cultivation such as Isaiah 40:11: "He tends his flock like a shepherd: He gathers the lambs in his arms and carries them close to his heart; he gently leads those that have young." This is exemplified by Jesus, who is described as "our Lord Jesus, that great Shepherd of the sheep" (Heb. 13:20). Those in this category have an overriding desire to make a significant impact for Christ and His kingdom. They are impassioned by statements such as John 4:34–38:

> "My food," said Jesus, "is to do the will of him who sent me and to finish his work. Do you not say, 'Four months more and then the harvest'? I tell you, open your eyes and look at the fields! They are ripe for harvest. Even now the reaper draws his wages, even now he harvests the crop for eternal life, so that the sower and the reaper may be glad together. Thus the saying 'One sows and another reaps' is true. I sent you to reap what you have not worked for. Others have done the hard work, and you have reaped the benefits of their labor."

Pastors drawn by this role often become operational leaders (more on this shortly).

But the second category, visionaries, have what church growth researcher Win Arn called "church growth eyes . . . a developed characteristic of individuals and churches who have achieved a sensitivity to seeing possibilities . . . ."[3] Pastors drawn by this leadership role usually become strategic leaders (more on this in a moment).

Often pastors and church leaders have a mixture of the two roles and may fluctuate between one or the other at various times in their ministerial journey. However, it is important to note the dissimilar nature of these roles: One seeks to build interpersonal camaraderie and intimacy; the other seeks to attain a physical forward-looking goal. In the former, intimacy is the purpose; and in the latter, the future goal is the purpose. Which is needed? They both are, but the wise church leader will employ each as the circumstance warrants and as his or her abilities allow.

Let's look a bit more at strategic leadership.

Pastors attracted to the ministry because of a vision to make a significant impact for Christ often exhibit strategic leadership. They are often passionate about their work, for they see the depravity of humankind and perceive how Christ provides the answer. Subsequently, they are often enthusiastic and energetic about reaching people for Christ. This passion can be misconstrued as a fervor for growth, size, or power. Such negative attributes can sneak in. However, what customarily motivates these individuals is the picture they envision of many people coming to know Christ. As such, visual and revelatory Scriptures hold great sway, and they can readily perceive the eventuality of Revelation 7:9–10: "a great multitude that no one could count, from every nation, tribe, people and language, standing before the throne and in front of the Lamb. They were wearing white robes and were holding palm branches in their hands. And they cried out in a loud voice: 'Salvation belongs to our God, who sits on the throne, and to the Lamb.'"

In the Change Process. Strategic leaders are the first to notice change is needed. This is because they are always looking ahead. To a degree they live in the future better than the present. They can be frustrating to work with if not accompanied by the tactical leader. Strategic leaders see the need for change and love discussing the rationale and theories of change.[4] They know what the change should look like, but they have trouble seeing the steps to get there. They are critical for the change process, for they look ahead and see where the church is going and needs to go. But they also are frustrating for other leaders, because strategic leaders know what the results should look like but are weak at envisioning the step-by-step process.

Characteristics. Strategic leadership is "future directed."[5] Strategic leaders often want people to move forward, and thus they are the first to start moving in new directions. Historian Martin Marty said they "are extremely sensitive to where people are, but are not content to leave them there."[6]

Other terms for strategic leaders are

1. *Visionaries* (George Barna,[7] Leith Anderson,[8] and Phil Miglioratti[9])
2. *Role One Leaders* (Phil Miglioratti)[10]
3. *Top management* (John Wimber, Eddie Gibbs)[11]
4. *Strong, authoritative, directive pastoral leadership* (C. Peter Wagner)[12]
5. *Upper-level management* (John Kotter)[13]
6. *Sodality leadership,* described as "vision setter, goal setter, strong leader, visionary, upper management" (Ralph Winter)[14]

Tactical Leaders

In History. Tactical leaders complement strategic leaders. Tactical leaders (from the Greek word *taktike* meaning *organize*) are those leaders skilled in the art of organizing, historically, an army. Such leaders are exact, accurate, and specific. Tactical leaders lead the forces once the battle begins. They focus on allocation, analysis, planning, evaluation, and adjustment once strategic leaders set the direction. Tactical leaders in the military are customarily ranked as colonels or below.

In Architecture. Returning to the architectural metaphor, the tactical leader is like a civil engineer.[15] He or she may receive a general idea of the architectural form from the homeowner or architect. But the tactical leader must compute the number of board-feet required, the utility needs, and the component costs associated with every element of the endeavor. The engineer puts together an infrastructure to undergird the artistic image the strategic leader has pictured.

In the Military. In the World War II invasions of North Africa, Sicily, Italy, and France, it would have been a mistake for generals far from the front to micromanage the invasion. Instead, planning, adaptive tactics, evaluation, allocation, personnel deployment, and adjustments for winning the invasion were the responsibility of tactical leaders once the battle had begun.

In the Church. Tactical leaders receive long-term goals from strategic leaders.[16] But tactical leaders contribute the critical and decisive tasks of planning, allocating, adjusting, and analyzing that bring about the future envisioned by a strategic leader. Tactical leadership fits these future plans into the ongoing life, tasks, and rhythms of what the church is doing presently. It "means fitting together of ongoing activities into a meaningful whole."[17] Tactical leadership makes the future, as seen by the strategic leader, happen in a unified manner. Management scholar Russell Ackoff's definition describes the role of tactical leaders where "planning is the design of a desired future and of effective ways of bringing it about."[18]

In the Change Process. Thus, a critical contribution that is often missing in our churches is the tactical leader who makes change happen—in a unifying way. Here we see the answer to Change Reaction 2, "our leaders are not good at bringing about change." Our leaders do not succeed at change because a critical link in making change happen is often missing: the tactical leader. Change does not succeed in its outcome because the necessary tactically skilled leaders who can implement unifying change are not involved. We shall see at the end of this chapter that we must integrate tactical leaders into the processes of change, or changes we seek will not make things better—only less unified.

Characteristics. Tactical leadership is an integrated skill. Tactical leaders wed the past, the present, and the future to move the church ahead. Tactical leaders grasp the strategic leader's vision of the future, but enjoy integrating these future plans into the ongoing and present life of the church. Tactical leaders also relish the planning process. They set timelines and allocate duties. They are delegators. They should not be confused with operational leaders, who do the work themselves. The tactical leader delegates fully and carefully evaluates the results.

Thus, tactical leaders are often pen and pencil (or stylus and PDA) people, who make copious notes as the strategic leader expounds upon the future. Tactical leaders create spreadsheets, flowcharts, and diagrams, and designate work teams. Tactical leaders know how to bring big long-term projects down into easy, doable steps.

Therefore, tactical leaders are the needed go-betweens to connect strategic leaders who grasp the big picture with operational leaders who get things done. Everyone appreciates tactical leaders, but regrettably they are usually outnumbered in our churches by strategic leaders and operational leaders. Consequently, the organization suffers.

Other terms for "tactical leaders" are

1. *Administrators* (Phil Miglioratti)[19]
2. *Role Two Leaders* (Phil Miglioratti)[20]
3. *Middle-level management* (D. Martin Butler and Robert Herman)[21]
4. *Middle management* (John Wimber and Eddie Gibbs,[22] and John Kotter[23])
5. "Enables others to achieve goals" (Richard Hutcheson)[24]
6. *Problem solvers* (Gary Yukl)[25]
7. *Modality leadership,* described as "enabler, team builder, ally, implementer" (Ralph Winter)[26]

Operational Leaders

In History. In the military operational leaders are the men and women who lead skilled teams on critical assignments. They have an immediate, urgent, and vital task to perform. They may not see where their efforts fit into the bigger picture, but they are the masters of relational leadership. They lead an intentional, personal effort to build a team of interdependent soldiers. While the key to strategic leadership is forecasting and theorizing, and the contribution of tacticians is precision and allocation, the skill of the operational leader is his or her connection with the team and ability to think creatively, improvise, adapt, and be successful.

In Architecture. These are the skilled craftsmen who build a house and give it the working components. They may be knowledgeable in a certain predefined field such as electrical, heating and cooling, framing, and so forth, because of the complexity of the task. And they like to see the immediate results of their hands. One operational leader told me, "I like to see immediate results from what I am doing. I do not have patience to wait for an outcome. That is why I am a painter." In contrast, the strategic leader may wait years to witness the culmination of a project, and thus may leap to a new idea before the first has come to fruition. The tactical leader is also patient in waiting for the project to be completed, but the tactical leader finds it rewarding to see that progress is being made and the end goal is getting nearer. However, for operational leaders, seeing immediate results in even small steps is one of the most rewarding parts of the process.

In the Military. In the military, the battle is usually won or lost because of operational leaders. Operational leaders foster teamwork, interdependence, improvisation, creativity, and unity toward a goal. They lead small groups (think of a platoon leader or a head usher) and only partially delegate responsibility. In the military these are the lieutenants and sergeants.

In the Church. My dad was a sergeant in the military, and initially an operational leader who led his small team of second-service ushers successfully. Like many operational leaders in our churches, Dad enjoyed getting the job done. I remember how fulfilled and satisfied he was after church, where he had faithfully discharged his duties with his team.

In the Change Process. During the change process these are the church leaders who get things done. They see things from the viewpoint of their task. If they are ushers, ushering seems like the most important job in the church. Still my dad, like many operational leaders today, knew the church was an organic organism of many functions and ministries (1 Cor. 12:12; Eph. 4:11–13). But Dad so enjoyed the task at hand that, at least for him and his giftings, this was the most important job imaginable. As a result he discharged his duties with speediness, precision, care, and results.

Characteristics. Operational leaders have the knowledge, skill, relational abilities, and dedication to get a job done. Once the parameters are defined and they see how their task fits into the bigger picture (they are helped in this by the tactical leader), the operational leader can accomplish almost anything. Anthropologist Margaret Mead observed, "Never doubt that a small group of committed citizens can change the world. Indeed, it is the only thing that ever has."[27] And, thus the contribution of the operational leader is critical to the change process.

Operational leaders often love their jobs so much that they do not see themselves "moving out" of this role in the foreseeable future.[28]

If the operational leader does not have the go-between of a tactical leader, however, the strategic leader's vision may be too imprecise to motivate the operational leader. Thus, we see once again, all three types of leadership are needed, but it is the go-between tactical leader who helps the operational leader move the strategic leader's vision forward.

Other terms for operational leaders are

1. *Workers* (Phil Miglioratti)[29]
2. *Role Three leaders* (Phil Miglioratti)[30]
3. *Foremen* (John Wimber and Eddie Gibbs)[31]

Strategic, Tactical, and Operational Leaders: A Comparison

Returning to our story, my father, Gerald, had been a successful sergeant in the military. He was known as loyal to his men, constantly looking out for their safety, but always leading them toward a visible goal within parameters that were provided to him. In such scenarios he excelled. Thus, as head usher of the second service he flourished as a leader of a ministry team.

The disaster began when the church leadership, largely unaware of distinctives between strategic, tactical, and operational leadership, rewarded my father with tactical leadership. Dad was an operational leader, and he enjoyed leadership that was defined by relationships and connectedness. Phil Miglioratti, describing strategic leadership as Role One leadership and tactical leadership as Role Two leadership, observed, "a mistake is made when these active dependable servants are 'rewarded' for their work by 'promoting' them to Role One or Two positions."[32]

Tactical leadership has more to do with allocation, analysis, creating tactical plans, and evaluation of effectiveness. Thus mechanical processes, of which as Gerald's son I am more inclined, did not attract my dad; nor were they aligned with his gifts. Dad was more personable than I will ever be, and he led a small team to success in World War II and at his church.

In Today's Church, Tactical Leaders Are Missing

Today congregants often don't know what to call a leader: a visionary, a realist, a planner, a strategist, a facilitator, a coach, or . . . ? I've noticed my students often lump church board leaders into two broad categories: board realists or board visionaries.

Actually my students have two-thirds of the categories right. There may be a better term for both groups. Those whom some students call real-ists should be called tactical leaders. These are leaders who see the impor-tant nuts-and-bolts implication of a new idea. They see the cost involved, the human power needed, and the steps required. They often appear not to be receptive to new ideas, because they see the elaborate infrastructure and cost that will be required. Thus they often butt heads with strategic leaders, because while strategic leaders see the future clearly, the tactical leaders see the immediate expenses more acutely.

Board visionaries are those strategic board leaders who see the bigger picture more sharply than they see the route to get there.

In Today's Church, Strategic Leaders Are Abundant

Regrettably, in the past twenty-five-plus years I have seen a decline in the important tactical leaders, and instead a proliferation of strategic leaders in our churches.[33] Most church pastors have read books about visionary leadership, and our seminaries have done a better job at fostering bigger-picture leaders. But an unfortunate outcome is that tactical church leaders are often missing in our congregations. Thus, churches cannot bring about change, because they are drowning under a deluge of strategic visionaries with big ideas and multiple strategies who have little idea of how to get there. We need a return in our churches to the development and deployment of tactical leaders.

Congregants we label visionaries should probably better be called strategic leaders. These are church leaders who see the bigger picture, though how to get there is cloudy. They capture a picture in their minds about what a new worship service can look like, but they are not as clear regarding the steps needed to attain it. While strategic leaders see the future, they often lack the analytical, precise, and number-crunching nature to move the process forward.

I believe many pastors go into the ministry because they can see the strategic, long-term picture. They relate to Jesus' admonition: "Do you not say, 'Four months more and then the harvest?' I tell you, open your eyes and look at the fields! They are ripe for harvest" (John 4:35). Strategic pastors can readily picture this image. They sermonize upon the importance of seeing the mission field, but when it comes to mounting a step-by-step strategy, analysis, and evaluation, they are usually quiet.

The problem is exacerbated because strategic leaders tend to hire associate and assistant pastors like themselves: strategic leaders. Thus, a church can be full of bigger-picture people (and thus an explosion of new ideas) without having the tactical leaders needed to draft the budget, organize the training, recruit the volunteers, and evaluate the results to make adjustments.

In Today's Church, Operational Leaders Are Often Wrongly Promoted to Tactical Leadership

On the other end of the spectrum are the many operational leaders like my dad, who keep a church humming. They enjoy the tasks they are given, often relational and operational in nature. But when these loyal saints are promoted to tactical leadership, they find their skill set does not match expectations. Rather than let the church leaders down (remember the operational leader's skills are relational), the operational leader in a tactical job will stop doing his or her job (often by resigning, but not in person) and quietly disappear (again to prevent further damage to relationships).

Again, the result is that our churches are missing tactical leaders. The tactical leader's gift for analysis, number-crunching, and in-depth planning is often seen as profane in comparison to the more pious duties of relationship building (operational leadership) or long-term envisioning (strategic leadership).[34] But all three are needed. We must promote both balance and holism in our management styles. We must discover, develop, and deploy the important tacticians in our churches to create a link between strategic thinkers and operational leaders.

DON'T GO ANY FURTHER WITHOUT TACTICAL LEADERS

It is permissible to read further, but please don't attempt to bring about any of the change processes in this book (or any other book) before you get your tactical leaders in place. As we have seen from the above, these practical and precise leaders are often overlooked in a sea of strategic visionaries and hardworking operational workers.

My observation from client case studies, is that roughly 20 percent of a congregation are tactical leaders, another 20 percent are strategic (for example, visionary) leaders, while the remaining 60 percent are operational leaders.

Italian economist Vilfredo Pareto is famed for saying that 80 percent of the value lies in 20 percent of the ingredients. His statement has been interpreted to infer that 20 percent of the people do 80 percent of the work. My experience with client case studies tends to confirm percentages close to Pareto's.

Thus, of that 20 percent doing the work, I have observed 8 percent are visionaries, 8 percent are workers, and 4 percent are tactical leaders.

If my field observations are correct, we are not getting 72 percent of our operational leaders involved. My hunch is that this is because we do not have enough tactical leaders to create suitable tactics and equip operational leaders for the task. Thus, congregational operational leaders will often lament that a church is too unorganized, when in reality they mean the church is missing key tactical leaders to organize the strategic leaders' visions.[35]

How to Help Leaders Succeed at "Bringing about Change"

Here, then, is a primary reason change is hard for churches to undertake and congregants lament, "Our leaders are not good at bringing about change." It is because we often do not have tactical leaders in place to successfully bring about change. It is tactical leaders who can orchestrate and oversee a step-by-step plan for change.

Church change is usually handled just by strategic leaders who make a case for seeing the bigger picture, without giving clear insight about how to get there. The result is that church operational leaders sense a gap between what the strategic leader pictures and how to get it done. So, operational leaders resist change because a clear route to get there has not been articulated.

Three things must happen to get tactical leaders involved:

1. Tactical leaders must be recruited and involved in the change process. Look for people who have the following characteristics:
   - They are planners.
   - They analyze needs and appropriate funds.
   - They create budgets.
   - They help obtain goal ownership from operational leaders.
   - They are hesitant about new ideas, because they can see the barriers and roadblocks that must be surmounted.
   - They are frustrated when strategic leaders try to micromanage the tactical process by offering too many ideas, corrections, or adjustments.
2. Tactical leaders must be allowed to drop their current responsibilities to tackle change.

- Because there is so much precision in tactical leaders' work, they cannot juggle as many projects as the strategic leader can envision. Remember, the strategic leader sees the bigger picture, but the actual mechanics are not as clear and require more effort to create.
- The detail needed in tactical planning prevents tactical leaders from being able to do a good job if they are juggling too many responsibilities.
- Tactical leaders must be allowed to drop some of their current responsibilities if these tasks are not aligned with the tactical leaders' tactical gifts, or if their duties are not as crucial to the future of the church as the new changes.

3. Tactical leaders need a rough plan.
   - They need a general plan they can follow, indigenize, and improve upon.
   - In this book, the plan for change is laid out in chapters 3–9.

A RECAP OF CHANGE REACTION 2: 'OUR LEADERS ARE NOT GOOD AT BRINGING ABOUT CHANGE'

Pastors hear "Our leaders are not good at bringing about change" because the tactical leaders, key go-betweens among the strategic and operational leaders, are missing from our churches. While both strategic and operational leaders are still needed, neither group has the requisite skills of analysis, step-by-step planning, number-crunching, and detail management to bring a change to fruition. This is the contribution of tactical leaders.

Typically in our churches we have three types of leaders.

Strategic Leaders

They see the need and the future. They have a limited idea of how to get there, but they have been exposed to various models to accomplish change. However, strategic leaders do not typically have the patience to analyze, fine-tune, crunch the numbers, tweak, perfect, evaluate, and adjust a strategy. Subsequently, strategic leaders often try to just apply (for example, franchise) a strategy that has worked elsewhere. The strategic leader may purchase step-by-step manuals for operational leaders. And while this is a good starting place, because tactical leaders who can adjust the methodology for the church's own unique scenario are not involved, the prefab strategy is often abandoned with people saying, "That doesn't work here." Again, the problem is not the strategic leaders or the operational leaders; they are both doing their jobs. The problem is created because an important link is missing: the tactical leaders and their organizational skills.

Tactical Leaders

They then become our crucial—and missing—link in effective change. If they are missing, change strategies are not adapted to the local context, and the process is unorganized.

Operational Leaders

In military jargon these are the "boots on the ground," the frontline workers who must adjust the tactics they are given. They are relational teams of workers who derive satisfaction from teammates and visible accomplishments. Operational leaders may also volunteer to be tactical leaders, because relationships are so important to them they do not want to see the strategic leader in a quandary. They may say something like "Pastor, I know you are in a spot here. So I'll help you out." If an operational leader says this, interview that person. Then, if this operational leader does not have the analytical, diagnostic, and methodical skills to create and manage an elaborate plan, graciously decline the offer. To thrust operational leaders into tactical positions will frustrate them, and eventually due to their gracious and relational nature, they will quietly fade away from their failed tactical task.

CHANGE IS DIFFICULT BECAUSE TACTICAL LEADERS ARE MISSING

Why then does change so often fail in congregations? It has been my observation that it is because strategic leaders (often pastors) try to orchestrate the tactical process. If a strategic leader in the role of pastor or department head tries to move the church forward with change, the congregants will become frustrated because the plan appears too nebulous and imprecise.

At the same time the strategic leader will expect the relationally oriented operational leaders to create a plan. And though the operational leaders are the key to the success of the process, their emphasis upon relationships usually trumps their interest in administrative details, budgeting, volunteer recruitment, and evaluation.

The answer is that change needs the critical link between strategic leader and operational leaders: tactical leadership. To succeed with change, it is important that at the outset the pastor develop those tactical leaders who can map out the change processes outlined in this book—and who will enjoy doing so.

QUESTIONS FOR GROUP STUDY

1. What kind of tasks do you enjoy? Circle only those letters that correspond to tasks you *greatly* enjoy.
   A. Dreaming about the future
   B. Preparing a budget

C. Getting to know a person you work with
D. Graphing a new plan
E. Analyzing what went wrong with a strategy
F. Creating a visual map of the planning process
G. Balancing your checkbook
H. Sharing about your family history
I. Reading books on new ideas
J. Attending seminars on creativity
K. Tackling a numerical problem
L. Reading books on history
M. Researching costs associated with a project
N. Creating a survey
O. Taking a survey
P. Leading fewer than twelve people on a project
Q. Recording the minutes of a meeting
R. Loading and adjusting new software on your computer
S. Designing ways to better communicate an idea
T. Relaxing by talking with friends about hobbies
U. Relaxing by talking with friends about what went wrong
V. Relaxing by dreaming with friends about new ideas
W. Working on a hobby with a few closer friends
X. Sharing your personal feelings with others
Y. Sharing your new ideas with others
Z. Getting a job done with a minimum of fuss

For each letter you circled, put a check in the corresponding box:

For each of the following letters you circled, put a check in this box.	For each of the following letters you circled, put a check in this box.	For each of the following letters you circled, put a check in this box
C, H, P, T, W, X, Z	B, D, E, F, G, K, M, N, Q, R, S, U	A, I, J, L, O, V, Y
Total: _____	Total: _____	Total: _____
Operational Leader	*Tactical Leader*	*Strategic Leader*
You may be primarily comfortable with a leadership style associated with the box that contains the most checkmarks.[36]		

2. Who are tactical leaders in your congregation? And what are they doing? Ask yourself:
   - How critical for the future of the organization are the current jobs these tactical leaders are undertaking?
   - Could these tactical leaders be used more effectively in other areas, perhaps helping the church move forward with some change? (This is a question that will be answered quickly by strategic leaders.)
   - Are these tactical leaders overworked and in danger of burnout? (This is a question that will be more promptly answered by operational leaders.)
3. What does this statement mean: "We must integrate tactical leaders into the processes of change, or changes we seek will not make things better—only less unified"?

What will you do to see this does not happen?

Name seven *tactical leaders* you will recruit and engage in reading this book.

Tactical Leader: Contact Information:

_____   _____

_____   _____

_____   _____

_____   _____

_____   _____

_____   _____

change reaction 3
do we really need to change?

the problem
some congregations believe change may be warranted but is elusive, thus they question the need for it.

do churches need to change?

"I don't know why they only come on Sunday night," declared this perplexed and frustrated pastor in his early sixties. "These young people should come on Sunday morning too. It's our time for worship, and it's our main service. If our youth pastor won't get them here Sunday morning, they are not really part of this congregation. The Bible says, 'Not forsaking the assembling of ourselves together, as the manner of some is; but exhorting one another: and so much the more, as ye see the day approaching'" (Heb. 10:25 KJV).

Pastor D, as he liked to be called, had grown a large church[1] comprised primarily of congregants from his generation. Yet, now the church had an assistant pastor who was reaching out to younger generations, something Pastor D had always prayed would happen. However, Pastor D was frustrated by their lack of attendance in the Sunday morning worship services. To him, this belied a lack of commitment. Yet, this assessment was distorted by his own generational expectations. The generation gap was hitting Pastor D hard, and soon both the assistant pastor and a sizable segment of the congregation under age thirty would be gone.

"Do we really need to change?" Pastor D lamented after the split. "It seems that change is needed, but it just drives people away."

THE NORTH AMERICAN CULTURAL MIX

North America is following the rest of the world and rapidly becoming a mixture of ethnicities, socioeconomic groupings, generations, and affinity groups. Let us look at a brief list of such groupings.

Ethnicities

These are groups customarily linked, but not exclusively, by biological connections. These biological connections are often due to genealogy or ancestry. Subsequently, ethnicities are often associated with an area of origin, for example, Irish (from the Republic of Ireland), Sri Lankans (from the Democratic Socialist Republic of Sri Lanka), and Yemenis (from the Republic of Yemen). Ethnic designations can also be provocative, and thus names are often evolving. My purpose here is not to offend, but to ensure the reader understands some concepts and examples of ethnicity.

Therefore, sizable North American examples could be (though again these are imprecise, and the names are evolving):

- Latin American
- Hispanic American
- African American
- Asian American
- Native American
- Anglo American

Still, country or area of origin may not clearly define an ethnic group. In a 2001 census the United Kingdom divided "Asian" (not without controversy)[2] into the following categories: Indian, Sri Lankan, Pakistani, Bangladeshi, and Other. And, according to the U.S. Central Intelligence Agency's *World Factbook*, China alone has fifty-plus ethnic groups.[3]

Thus, while ethnicity gives us a broad category from which to view a culture, there are many cultures within most ethnicities. Thus, these examples are given only to acquaint the reader with the types of cultural categories I am referring to when employing the word *ethnicity*.

Socioeconomic Groupings[4]

These are groups that have similar interests and behaviors due to their current socioeconomic level. These groupings are designated by, but are not limited to, occupation, education, and income. In North America sociologists have proposed various designations and sub-designations for socioeconomic levels. One of the oldest and most basic is working class, middle class, and capitalist (or upper) class.[5] Again, these designations are objectionable and awkward for many people, including this author. But the purpose of recounting them here is to help the reader see the economic mosaic of the North American cultural landscape.

Hickey and Thompson[6] have created widely accepted socioeconomic categorizations that can be helpful for gaining an overall appreciation of these groupings:

- Upper socioeconomic level (1–5 percent of the North American population)—characterized by power over economic, business, and political organizations and institutions
- Middle socioeconomic levels:
  - Upper middle socioeconomic level (15 percent of the North American population)—customarily white-collar workers who hold graduate degrees who have a significant degree of flexibility and autonomy in their work
  - Lower middle socioeconomic level (33 percent of the North American population)—customarily white-collar workers with some college education; enjoy a degree of flexibility and autonomy at work, but not as much as the upper middle socioeconomic level
- Lower socioeconomic levels:
  - Working socioeconomic level (30 percent of the North American population)—both white- and blue-collar workers whose jobs are distinguished by low job security, inadequate pay, and worries about losing health insurance
  - Lower socioeconomic level (15 percent of the North American population)—Typically go through cycles of part-time and full-time jobs and often must work more than one job to provide for their needs

Church leaders will recognize that socioeconomic levels readily create community and lifestyle cultures.

Generations

Generations are increasingly becoming important cultures within North American society. Together with colleague Kent Hunter, I have written an exhaustive look at how churches can reach out to younger generations without alienating older members.[7]

Some may wonder why these generations are so pronounced, when in the early 1900s this was not the case. Largely due to niche marketing of the post-World War II era, different consumer preferences have been cultivated for different generations. While prior to 1945, a son might be expected to use the same shaving cream as his father, and a daughter use the same laundry soap as her mother; after World War II billions of advertising dollars were spent trying to get different generations to adopt different preferences in everything from soap to fashion, and soft drinks to automobiles. The result is that different generations have different styles and tastes in aesthetics, such as fashion, music, art, automobiles, and even soft drinks.

Similarly, why did the nineteen-year demarcations for generations arise? This is primarily a product of the field of sociology, where a nineteen-year span covers the rough age span of childbearing. In addition, sociologists feel nineteen-year demarcations cover a range of societal and cultural forces that shape a generation's outlook and preferences. As you can see in figure 3.1, these nineteen-year spans are helpful but not precise. Today, there are many sub-generational groupings. But to keep this discussion from becoming too complex, I will describe only a few sub-generations.

Let's look at a brief overview of the various North American generations in figure 3.1

BIRTH YEARS OF GENERATIONS

Birth Years	Age in 2008	Designation
1945 and before	63+	Builders
1946–1964	44–62	(Baby) Boomers
1965–1983	25–43	Generation X
	(34–43)	(Leading Edge Gen-X)
	(25–33)	(Postmodern Gen-X)
1984–2002	6–24	Generation Y

Generations are placed in nineteen-year categories due to a theory that global events and experiences during such spans of time will predetermine people born in those years to act in similar ways. These spans of time also have different labels to generally describe each. Below is a short overview.[8]

The Builder Generation, built the United States into a worldwide military and economic power. Influenced by Northern European heritage and art, they often honor God with the craftsmanship of their hands. Thus, their churches tend to be architectural and aesthetic masterpieces, using fine woods, artistic garnishes (such as colorful stained glass), and artistic masonry. They also prefer lecturing in sermonizing, organizational stability, and predictability in liturgy.

Baby Boomer, often abbreviated to *boomer*, comes from Old-West parlance. A boom town was a city that sprang up overnight due to the discovery of gold or some other precious commodity. The term was borrowed to describe the boom in births that occurred after World War II as North America enjoyed unparalleled prosperity and peace. Their churches are often shrines to flexibility, where a sanctuary may be quickly and easily converted to a basketball court after Sunday morning services and converted back again to a sanctuary by Sunday evening. They prefer sermons that have highly applicable lessons, flexibility in their organizations, and variety in the liturgy.

Generation X, sometimes shortened to *Xers*, was given this unlikely moniker by boomers who sought to describe a perceived nihilism and negativism in boomer offspring. However, Generation X is not as negative or pessimistic as boomers suspect. In fact, Generation X is not only religious, but on a quest to make churches more relational, less program-orientated, and more emotionally healthy.[9] They prefer interaction and questioning during sermons, organizational change, and experimentation in liturgy. Here's an example of their emphasis on change. A popular TV game show that aired on the Music TV (MTV) channel was, at the height of its popularity, suddenly cancelled. The game show, called *Remote Control*, was the highest rated and most watched program on MTV. Critics were dumbfounded. Boomers who watched it were outraged. To this uproar, the executives at MTV responded that they did not want anything to become predictable or repetitive on MTV. Thus, even though the show was a moneymaker and popular, innovation and creativity trumped money and status. At the height of its popularity, MTV canceled its most popular show, in hopes of fostering further creativity and innovation. Now, ask yourself, how long have boomer game shows, such as *The Price is Right* and *Wheel of Fortune*, been on the air? See the difference between generations?

Within Generation X, I have observed two subcategories:

- **Leading-edge Xers** are the older Gen-Xers, whom I thus designate because they forged their generational culture on the heels of a boomer generation. As such, many of these leading edge Xers mirror boomer preferences and predilections. Not surprisingly, many leading edge Xers relate closely to and even look like younger boomers.
- **Postmodern Xers** is the second subcategory of Generation X. They tend to be more culturally distant from boomers, and thus often reject boomer sensibilities and perspectives. For example, boomers are influenced by modernist philosophies, which highly respect education. Postmodern Xers are influenced more by the experience-orientated philosophies of postmodernism, and thus they emphasize experience. An example would be Mike Yankoski and Sam Purvis, who as college students left school for five months to live on the streets as homeless persons.[10] While studying homelessness in college, they decided they wanted experience to inform their knowledge. Unlike boomers, who might read a gaggle of books on homelessness, postmodern Xers see experience as the preferred learning venue. Thus, postmodern Xers often are at odds with boomers over what they see as a boomer emphasis on education, perfection, and bigness.[11]

Generation Y is still developing cultural preferences and predilections. However, so far it mirrors Generation X in much the same way that leading edge Xers mirror boomers. While time will tell how cultural behaviors, ideas, and attitudes will develop, at this point the older Gen-Yers appear to be more a subset of Generation X than a radically different generation.

Affinity Groups

In addition to the myriad of ethnicities, socioeconomic groupings, and generations, are a wide variety of affinity groups, so labeled because of a common affinity, passion, interest, pastime, fashion, activity, music, and/or pursuit. Affinity groups identify with one another; and others identify them as a group. Since there are too many to describe, I'll tender a few examples.

Motorcycle Riders. These enthusiasts can be blue-collar workers or white-collar professionals. But, they have the same affinity for freedom and fast machines. Many ride Harley-Davidson motorcycles, but others ride Japanese and European sport bikes, vintage motorcycles, Indian motorcycles, dirt bikes, and café racers. They acknowledge each other as they pass on the highway, often giving a salutary wave. Observers know them as well, yet usually are not so friendly. Their affinity is summed up in the well-known Biker's Creed, whose nineteenth point is, "I am not a part-time biker. I am a biker when and wherever I go. I am proud to be a biker and hide my chosen lifestyle from no one. I ride because I love freedom, independence, and the movement of the ground beneath me. But most of all, I ride to better understand myself, my machine, the lands in which I ride, and to seek out and know other bikers as myself."[12]

The NASCAR Nation. Observers and participants in North America's homegrown stock car challenge called NASCAR make up another affinity group. They signal to each other their loyalty by numbers representative of their hero's car. NASCAR (National Association for Stock Car Auto Racing), has fanatical devotees who show up by the tens of thousands at three series of races: the NEXTEL Cup, the Busch Series, and the Craftsman Truck Series. Though their fan base began in the southwestern United States in the mid-1900s, it now extends to automotive aficionados across North America.

Goths. These are often young people who dress in predominately dark attire and prefer the edgy, rhythmic music of alternative-metal groups. Many sport multiple facial and body piercings, along with an array of tattoos. Typically young people, their hair and fashion may cause alarm or unease among their more proper boomer progenitors. Often these young people feel alienated and disenfranchised. Their bodies often become the canvas upon which to paint their frustration and irritation with the life they have been handed. They identify with Paul's statement about the wealthy and successful (though superficial) Corinthian church. Paul remarked with his tongue in cheek,

> Already you have all you want! Already you have become rich! You have become kings—and that without us! How I wish that you really had become kings so that we might be kings with you! For it seems to me that God has put us apostles on display at the end of the procession, like men condemned to die in the arena. We have been made a spectacle to the whole universe, to angels as well as to men. We are fools for Christ, but you are so wise in Christ! We are weak, but you are strong! You are honored, we are dishonored! . . . We work hard with our own hands. When we are cursed, we bless; when we are persecuted, we endure it; when we are slandered, we answer kindly. Up to this moment we have become the scum of the earth, the refuse of the world (1 Cor. 4:8–13).

Not surprising, a young growing church reaching out to Goths in urban Denver chose the name "Scum of the Earth" for their church. They did so with tongue in cheek as did Paul, and as a statement of their feelings of disenfranchisement from successful boomer churches nearby.[13] Those who feel such names are too controversial should remember many denominational and church names were initially derogatory and/or controversial, including Methodist and Baptist.

From the above examples we see that in each circumstance symbols, language, and style allow members of each group to identify those within their group and those outside it. In addition, these artifacts of style, language, and symbols allow outsiders to identify the group. We shall now see that each of the above groupings is best described as a culture.

THE CHARACTER OF A CULTURE

Christian anthropologist Paul Hiebert has described a culture as an "integrated system of learned patterns of behavior, ideas and products characteristic of a society."[14] It is important here to note each of Hiebert's three distinctions: "patterns of behavior, ideas and products."

Behavior

Behavior refers to action patterns that are characteristic of a cultural grouping. The inclination for motorcyclists to embrace the freedom, and even danger, of open road riding is a distinguishing behavior. The behavior of Goths to embrace raucous hard-driving music and mosh pits where participants *mosh* or *shank* as they push off and shove one another, is another. The behavior of the builder generation to worship with craftsmanship and skill, while boomers honor God with their quest for bigness and quality, attests to different generational behaviors.

Ideas

Ideas indicates that each culture has a certain view of life and relationships, though within that view may be many viewpoints. For instance, Goths have a collective and pessimistic view of the world. They see the world has handed them a rough and brutal situation, so they feel they must be equally tough and independent to survive. This desire for freedom and independence from the negative aspects of their environment can be a touchstone for Christians who are Goth-sensitive to explain that Jesus offers the power to rise above circumstance.

Another example of divergent ideas is the attitude of postmodern Generation Xers, who often see the world as degenerating into hopeless chaos and thus embrace a more pessimistic outlook than their optimistic boomer parents. Compare the lyrics of boomer musicians Paul McCartney and his colleague John Lennon, with the postmodern Xer lyrics of John Mayer. Lennon and McCartney wrote—

Getting Better by Paul McCartney and John Lennon.[15]
> Me used to be angry young man.
> Me hiding me head in the sand.
> You gave me the world I finally heard.
> I'm doing the best that I can.
> To admit it's getting better, A little better all the time

Waiting on the World to Change by John Mayer.[16]
> Now we see everything that's going wrong with the world,
> And those who lead it.
> We just feel like we don't have the means,
> To rise above and beat it.
> So we keep waiting, waiting on the world to change.

Products

Products are what Paul Hiebert calls the physical artifacts created by a culture, such as fashion, literature, poetry, and so forth. The colorful banners, stickers, hats, and T-shirts of the NASCAR Nation that proudly cheer on their heroes are products of a culture. When a NASCAR fan with 23 on his hat sees a stranger with the same number on his bumper, there is an immediate connection. And the sign "In Memory of #3" brings a moment of silent reflection and sadness to all fans who remember the untimely passing of NASCAR great Dale Earnhardt Sr. In contrast to the bright and happy colors of NASCAR, the dark and somber products of Goth music and dress hint at the bleak and disheartened outlook of many young people who identify with this subculture.

CULTURE: CORRUPT BUT CONVERTIBLE

When we look at the variety of cultures, we often see elements that are counter to the teachings of Christ. The pessimistic outlook of many postmodern Xers is different from the biblical outlook that encourages us to "Speak to one another with psalms, hymns and spiritual songs. Sing and make music in your heart to the Lord, always giving thanks to God the Father for everything, in the name of our Lord Jesus Christ" (Eph. 5:19–20) and the reminder that "Every good and perfect gift is from above, coming down from the Father of the heavenly lights, who does not change like shifting shadows. He chose to give us birth through the word of truth, that we might be a kind of firstfruits of all he created" (James 1:17–18). Thus we see that many elements of every culture need the good news.

At the same time, some elements of these cultures are not in opposition to the good news, but rather support it. Generation X's solidarity with the poor and desire to help the needy is consistent with biblical teachings in Matthew 22:37–39 and James 1:27. Evangelist Billy Graham said, "Jesus taught that we are to take regeneration in one hand and cup of cold water in the other."[17]

What then are we to do when certain elements of a culture go against the Bible and other elements support it? Anthropologist Charles Kraft responds that culture is "corrupt, but convertible."[18] He emphasizes that though "Christ is above culture," Christ is also "working through culture."[19] And, "God chooses the cultural milieu . . . as the arena for his interaction with people,"[20] for example, Jesus' taking on the form of a human being to communicate with us (Phil. 2:6–11).

Thus the church must analyze a culture and put the good news into terms a culture can understand to help people of that culture have a conversion experience. While we must remain above the evil aspects of culture, we still must use cultural *behavior*, *ideas*, and *products* (when they do not go against the biblical teachings) to interact and communicate with different cultures.

CULTURE SIFTING

Though culture has some elements that are against the teachings of Christ, a culture is still the milieu in which we must communicate our message. Subsequently, conscientious Christians will have to sift through the various behaviors, ideas, and products of a culture. This means Christians who are missionaries to other cultures must ascertain what cultural elements are impure and reject them, while retaining elements that agree with the teachings of Christ.

Let's return to our postmodern Generation X illustration. Postmodern Generation Xers are sensitive to the needs of the poor and seek to alleviate human suffering. This is consistent with Christ's message. At the same time, there is a habit of some postmodern Xers to live together before marriage, and this goes against the biblical prohibition of adultery. Thus, the church that seeks to communicate the good news with postmodern Xers must sift through these cultural behaviors, ideas, and products and filter out that those are inconsistent with Christ and retain those that support Christianity. As such, premarital living together would be out, but solidarity with the poor would be in. Fuller seminary professor Eddie Gibbs puts it this way: God "acts redemptively with regard to culture, which includes judgment on some elements, but also affirmation in other areas, and a transformation of the whole."[21]

The mosaic of cultures today requires a three-phase engagement with that culture:

1. Carefully investigate elements of a culture.
2. Sift out elements that go against the good news, retain those that affirm it.
3. Using the elements that remain, communicate the good news with that culture.

COMMUNICATING THE GOOD NEWS ACROSS CULTURAL DIVIDES

This author wholeheartedly agrees with Charles Kraft's argument that the source for our message must be the Bible.[22] The Bible provides God's revelation to humankind about our shortcomings, our needs, our salvation, and our destiny. Because the message has eternal implications, we must handle it diligently and carefully. Kraft says that while the receiver of our good news is the goal of our communication, the key to successful communication is the secondary source that lies between the good news and the person who is the goal of our communication. Let's picture this relationship.

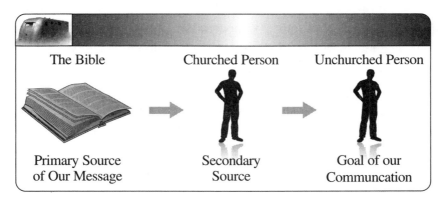

| The Bible | Churched Person | Unchurched Person |
| Primary Source of Our Message | Secondary Source | Goal of our Communcation |

The initial Bible message often goes through a key secondary source. Here is where communication can break down. If the secondary source, usually an evangelical Christian, does not know how to sift a culture and explain the good news in the behaviors, ideas, and products of the target culture, the message will not be understood by the person unacquainted with church culture.

The problem is exacerbated when the secondary source and the goal of our communication come from different cultures. Because different behavior, ideas, and products exist in each culture, the message will usually not make sense if the key secondary source, the person in the middle, does not understand a culture before he or she tries to communicate with it.

Why is this communication across cultural divides so difficult? It is because today our churches have become separate cultures themselves, with their own behavior, ideas, and products. Let's look at an example of church culture.

Behavior

Church people customarily worship on Sunday morning, and this becomes an expected behavior. Postmodern Xers in their twenties and without children often prefer to worship on Sunday evenings. Builder Generation church leaders who are comfortable and content with Sunday morning services will look at this postmodern desire as unusual, if not absurd. Even if the Sunday night worship option is allowed, builder church leaders will often see it though their builder-Christian culture and never fully embrace it as a *bona fide* worship alternative.

The problem has arisen because church leaders have not noticed their long history in the church has led to the formation of a subtle church culture, and that they have become less flexible because of their own preferences.

As a result, evangelism often stalls. This happens because the goal of our communication, those unchurched people in another culture, look at our message and find it inconsistent with the positive elements of their culture. Subtle cultural barriers can hinder our communication and blur our message.

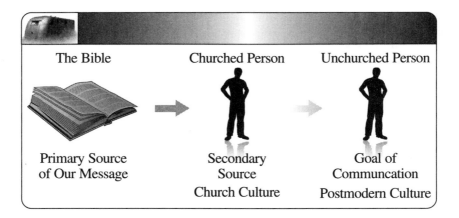

The Bible   Churched Person   Unchurched Person

Primary Source   Secondary   Goal of
of Our Message   Source   Communcation
    Church Culture   Postmodern Culture

The illustration that began this chapter was a true story about how the young people of a thriving church left and started their own congregation because the pastor was looking at Gen-X attendance through his own cultural lenses. Pastor D knew that for him and for many others, Sunday mornings had been the preferred time for worship. And subtly, but steadily, over the years a cultural *behavior* had arisen among his generation that regular Sunday morning attendance indicated a growing spiritual life. And thus visible attendance on Sunday morning became a point of conflict between two cultures—a builder-Christian culture and a postmodern-Christian culture.

The verse Pastor D quoted, Hebrews 10:25, was appropriate, and states, "Not forsaking the assembling of ourselves together, as the manner of some is; but exhorting one another: and so much the more, as ye see the day approaching." Pastor D had for years used this phrase to remind errant builders to be in church on Sunday mornings. Eventually, through use and custom, this Scripture came to be seen as an admonition for the primacy of Sunday morning attendance.

Let us look at Hebrews 10:25 again in the New International Version, which brings out more clearly the intent of the King James wording: "Let us not give up meeting together, as some are in the habit of doing, but let us encourage one another—and all the more as you see the Day approaching." Here we see that the admonition is to "not give up meeting together, as some are in the habit of doing." The message is about regular fellowship, worship, and Bible study with other Christians. And, this certainly takes place during Sunday morning worship. But for the postmodern Xers it took place during Sunday evening worship. This Scripture is not about a certain day or time, even though due to long-standing cultural usage it has been attached to one particular time as it was to Pastor D.

The result is that the message gets fuzzy as it crosses cultural boundaries. Notice how the right arrow in figure 3.3 is now depicted as grayer, less distinct, even fuzzy. This is what happens to our message as it crosses cultural barriers if we are not careful to study, sift, and communicate cultural behavior, ideas, and products. Let's look now at ideas and products in the context of church culture.

Ideas

Postmodern Xers have a deep concern for the poor and needy, as did Jesus and His disciples (for example, Matt. 22:37–39; James 1:27). This is also a part of the builder and boomer church's mission. However, evangelical boomer churches have a checkered past in bringing about social action. Christian historian Sherwood Wirt said the evangelical church's attempt to meet physical, emotional, and safety needs of God's creation "must be judged a failure."[23] Therefore, boomer and builder churches can learn and benefit from interaction with socially conscientious postmodern Xers. But, Xers notice our ineffectiveness in taking care of society's needy, and thus we must be honest and admit our shortcomings, or the message we are trying to communicate may be drowned out by our perceived arrogance.

Products

How each culture crafts and uses products will either hinder or enhance our transmission of the good news. Today's postmodern Xers have grown up in a computerized environment with instant communication over the

Internet or text-messaging phones. Many younger generations are probably unsure of what a cassette-tape recorder is. They will want sermons, music, and training via Podcast over the Internet, or downloadable from an online audio distribution site such as Apple's iTunes.[24] The church that uses primarily only its own cultural products, for instance cassette-tape machines for builders or audio CDs for boomers, will find itself not communicating with younger generations.

The church that persists in using its own time-tested methods exclusively will only reach more people of its own generation. While there is nothing wrong with reaching primarily your own generation or culture, in most circumstances there will come a time when this will create a weakness in the church. For example

1. A boomer church will eventually die if it does not reach younger generations.
2. An African American church may pass away if African Americans are declining in a neighborhood, and it does not reach out to the Asian American culture that is growing in the same neighborhood.

THE ANSWER TO CHURCH SURVIVAL: A MULTICULTURAL CONGREGATION

Longevity and Strength

Multicultural churches may be multiethnic, multigenerational, multisocioeconomic, multi-affinity, or a combination of these cultures. Many so-called multi-site congregations are in essence multicultural congregations.[25]

In North America's growing mix of ethnicities, generations, and affinity groups—cultures all—we must be prepared to foster multicultural churches for strength and longevity.

Multicultural churches foster larger congregations with greater pooled resources. Admittedly, unity becomes more difficult as size increases (antidotes will be discussed shortly). But, organic small groups and clusters of these groups as seen in England's largest Anglican congregation, St. Thomas' Church of Sheffield, are proof that sub-congregations and small groups can be the glue to bind a large congregation together.[26]

In addition, a greater variety of talents and skills are available and used in a large multicultural church. Due to cultural movement and travel, the predominant culture in a community may not remain that way for long. This is always true for generational cultures. Thus, the only way to ensure longevity in the face of cultural movement and passage is to build a church on a multicultural outreach strategy. This requires the church to deal regularly with change due to cultural differences and permutations.

Culturally Varied Worship

But why do people prefer worship in culturally different ways? Different cultures have different behaviors, ideas, and products. Because worship comprises behaviors, ideas, and products, differences are evident in the style of worship, music, and preaching with which each culture feels most comfortable.

For example, a Builder Generation might like hymns and a lecture format in the sermon. Boomers might prefer modern and lively country-inspired music, and a preacher who walks into the audience and engages the listeners. Generation X may like slow, reflective, and thoughtful music. In addition, Generation Xers might want sermons they can interrupt to ask the preacher questions or suggest their own perspectives.[27] A worship service that regularly blends such cultural styles creates an uneven, and to some unfulfilling, cultural experience.

Different behaviors, ideas, and products also occur in ethnicities. In many Latin American cultures, for example, having your children present with you in the worship service shows concern for your children. While in other ethnicities, children are expected to be sequestered in the nursery or children's church.

Again, different cultural behaviors, ideas, and products mean multicultural churches should have varied worship expressions if they want most congregants to be engaged in worship, as well as to provide relevant bridges congregants can use to introduce their friends to Christ.[28]

Organizing the Multicultural Church

E Pluribus Unum: out of many, one. Organizing the multicultural church requires some separation, especially in aesthetics and styles, but also unity in message and interaction. In other words, while worship and spiritual engagement are usually influenced by styles of music and liturgy (or lack of it), there must also be regular times for unifying the congregation. Let's look at an example of the multicultural church that has flourished in the Southern Baptist Convention for over half a century.

Figure 3.4 is the organizational structure of many Southern Baptist churches in the southern United States who have been reaching out effectively to Hispanic as well as Anglo cultures. Today in many metropolitan communities, the multiethnic church is prevalent, having saved many aging congregations by fostering an influx and eventual substitution by a new culture.

The *multigenerational* church is another multicultural variation, and might look like figure 3.5.

Different cultures are different sub-congregations. These smaller churches within a church (as depicted in figures 3.4 and 3.5) are sub-congregations within the larger congregational body.[29] Church growth scholar George Hunter suggests that most congregations today are already "congregations of congregations."[30] Yet, to not recognize this is one of the most prevalent yet perilous mistakes any church leader can make.

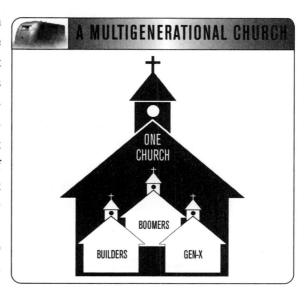

A MULTIGENERATIONAL CHURCH

ONE CHURCH

BOOMERS

BUILDERS   GEN-X

Thus the keys to growing a multicultural church are:

1. **Reach out by organizing as many sub-congregations as feasible.** Do not be afraid of sub-congregations; offer as many as you can. A church that can offer a postmodern Xer worship celebration in addition to a boomer modern service and a builder traditional service will reach more people in a community than one blended service.[31] This is because each culture worships more easily and comfortably in the music and aesthetics of its own culture. While some of my clients tell me their church truly enjoys blending the musical styles of traditional and modern music, I usually find this is really a style the churchgoers have come to like. It is an artificial style, but still appreciated. The problem is that this blended style aggravates some people who have strong style preferences. Blended worship has just about enough of everything to make just about everybody mad. Thus blended styles are not evangelistically powerful, for they are a Christian culture mutation that unchurched people will find abnormal, if not uncomfortable. To illustrate this, just ask yourself, how many radio stations do you

find that follow a classical musical composition by Bach or Mendelssohn with a rock song by the Beatles or Paul Simon?

2. **Unify a church by getting the same message out to all sub-congregations.** This means that if possible the same sermon should be used in all venues. This creates the same message to all congregants, regardless of culture. If this is not possible, then the message carriers (preachers, teachers, and so forth) must meet regularly for prayer, mentoring, and study to ensure the congregation is hearing a unified message. In my client base, failure to do this is the primary cause of factions and group exits.

3. **Unify the church by having inter-sub-congregational events on a regular basis.** When it comes to holding regular and engaging unity celebrations, most churches do a poor job. I know of one multicultural church—reaching Anglos, Hispanics, and Asians—that has only one unified worship gathering each year. And, because it is largely planned by the Anglo leaders, it is poorly attended by Hispanic and Asian members. It is necessary to offer a unity event, planned by representatives from *all* sub-congregations, at least four times a year. More often is better. St. Thomas' Church in Sheffield hosts one every Sunday night, to unify their nine sub-congregations.

Congregations have been organized as multi-congregational congregations since the 1950s. Daniel Sanchez led the Southern Baptist Churches into embracing various ethnic sub-congregations.[32] Churches in some of the more multiethnic areas such as Southern California have been doing this since the 1960s. But, the time is upon us when such holistic and multicultural ministry will be needed in almost every community. If you are not planning for change to accommodate this now, your fellowship will most likely die—at least in its present location or character.

QUESTIONS FOR GROUP STUDY

1. Discuss the variety of the following in your community. List different behavior, ideas, and products of each.
   - Ethnicities
   - Generations
   - Affinity groups
2. How divided were ethnicities in North America 150 years ago? How divided are they today?
   - What do you think caused this?
   - What do you think the next 150 years will hold?
3. Cultural sub-congregations often split from a mother church.
   - What does this do to the mother church?
   - What message does it send to the community?
   - And what message does it send to the group that leaves the church?
4. How have you accommodated different cultures, such as generational cultures, in the past?
   - Have you hosted once a month services for them, allowed them to have part of the regular service, or _____?
   - Has this created less controversy or more?
5. Bring a local newspaper to your meeting. Before you do, circle all of the affinity groups, generational cultures, and ethnicities mentioned in the paper.
   - What does this tell you about the cultural makeup of your community?
   - What must you do as a church to address this?

part two

A BIBLICAL THEOLOGY OF CHANGE

change reaction 4

if God doesn't change, why should we?

the problem

congregations are skeptical about change in the church because they understand that God's character is unchanging.

God is unchanging in four areas

When consulting with churches on long-term growth plans, I ask church leaders to confidentially list their church's strengths. I also ask them to write a paragraph about each strength, so I can fully understand what they are describing.

In over a decade of asking this question, I have discovered the responses fall into fifteen general categories. I've ranked these in order of occurrence, the most frequent categories appearing first:[1]

1. Our church is a caring church.[2]
2. Our church is a friendly church.
3. Our church emphasizes biblical teachings.
4. Our church leaders are hard working and care about the church.
5. Our church is where I find most of my friends.
6. Our church cares for families.
7. Our church cares for the needy.
8. Our church cares for all generations.
9. Our church cares for all people, regardless of culture.
10. Our church has a strong Sunday school program.
11. Our church has a strong youth program.
12. Our church has a strong children's ministry.
13. Our church has a good facility.
14. Our church has a strong music ministry.
15. Our church has a strong teaching ministry.

This ranking unleashes a whole realm of questions. Why is a biblical emphasis third? Shouldn't care for the needy be higher? Aren't the first two categories focused mostly inward toward church attendees rather than outward toward the unchurched? Though these are engaging questions, regrettably they are beyond the scope of this book.[3] Rather, for the present discussion these categories give us a picture of what strengths congregants see in their churches.

Likewise, it is important to note the rankings. Programs, strategies, specific plans, detailed tactics, and ministries are not at the top of the list. Though specific strategies appear from time to time, they appear farther down. Programs and specific ministries consistently do not rank in the top nine categories of perceived congregational strengths.[4]

What is more interesting is that attitudes and congregational qualities (1–9) are at the top of the list. Underlying and foundational qualities appear to be highly ranked, more than individual programs or specific ministries. While programs, ministries, and strategies may come and go, congregants put underlying, abiding, and foundational attitudes and essential character qualities at the top of their lists.

Congregants may perceive a church as more than a montage of popular programs, familiar ministries, or trendy strategies. Rather, the glue of a local church appears to be those enduring character qualities that resurface in different endeavors, ministries, and plans. At the end of this chapter we shall return to this observation and see that this points us toward a theology of biblical change.

WHAT IS A THEOLOGY OF CHANGE, AND WHO NEEDS IT?

Lay Leaders as Theologians?

Looking at congregational strengths cannot be our only starting point for an investigation into God's attitude toward change. We need to also consider carefully God's perception on change. The study of God's perspective on a topic is called *theology*—a combination of the Greek words *theos*, meaning "god," and *logos*. *Logos* has a broad and rich meaning that emphasizes (among other things) the study, scrutiny, and concept of some topic. Thus *theo-logy* is the scrutiny of God's viewpoint on some subject.

In many realms, including the one in which I commonly circulate, the Bible is considered to be the primary source for understanding God's viewpoint on various topics. Thus, this book's investigation into a theology of change will be a biblical quest.

Regrettably, church volunteers and lay leaders often feel theology is the exclusive (and perhaps elusive) realm of the professional minister. However, whenever any person considers God's perspective on a topic, that person is conducting theology—scrutiny of God's viewpoint on a subject.[5] Today, most church volunteers find themselves conducting theology to teach a Sunday school class, lead a Bible study, or prepare a devotional. The realm of theology is no longer the exclusive domain of professional staff, but a learning opportunity for all Christians.

I wholeheartedly agree with this trend. I believe this is what Jesus encouraged when He quoted Old Testament passages to His hearers to stimulate their investigation into God's viewpoint. For example, when Jesus encountered a Samaritan woman by a well in John 4:1–26, He did not seem surprised or offended that she wanted to engage in a theological discussion.

> "Sir," the woman said, "I can see that you are a prophet. Our fathers worshiped on this mountain, but you Jews claim that the place where we must worship is in Jerusalem."

Verses 19–20: In response, Jesus did not chastise her for this theological question, but used this interest to stimulate theological inquiry into the meaning of true worship.

> Jesus declared, "Believe me, woman, a time is coming when you will worship the Father neither on this mountain nor in Jerusalem. You Samaritans worship what you do not know; we worship what we do know, for salvation is from the Jews. Yet a time is coming and has now come when the true worshipers will worship the Father in spirit and truth, for they are the kind of worshipers the Father seeks. God is spirit, and his worshipers must worship in spirit and in truth."
>
> The woman said, "I know that Messiah" (called Christ) "is coming. When he comes, he will explain everything to us."
>
> Then Jesus declared, "I who speak to you am he."

Verses 22–24. Jesus encouraged the Samaritan woman to consider Old Testament Scriptures (2 Kings 17:28–41 and Isa. 2:3) and theologically reflect upon the differences that had driven apart Samaritans and Jews.

Verses 25–26. His goal was to provide guidance that might lead her to a theological conclusion: that He was the Messiah (vv. 25–26). That she was a woman of mixed heritage in a patriarchal world did not seem to bother Jesus in the least. He seems to encourage and enjoy this child of God grappling with theological inquiry and conclusion.

When Church Volunteers Carry out Theology, the Church Grows

Roger Finke of Penn State and Rodney Stark of the University of Washington are respected management professors. As interested laymen they studied two-hundred-plus years of North American church growth to uncover what factors influenced church growth. One conclusion is that when theology is conducted by volunteers and clergy outside the cloistered halls of seminaries, the church has grown.[6] Harvey Cox, professor of divinity at Harvard University, gleefully observed, "Theology is being done today—in curious places, under unusual sponsorship, by unauthorized persons, unnoticed by those who read only the right journals."[7]

Thus, if considering theology is permissible (per Jesus' example above), productive (per Finke and Stark), and pervasive (per Cox), we should encourage it today, especially in regard to such thorny issues as change.

A purpose in this book is to foster a partnership between church volunteers and clergy that will investigate God's perspective (a biblical theology) on change. Therefore, let us look at God's Word and engage in a layperson-pastoral partnership to see what the Scriptures have to say about change.

GOD IS UNCHANGING

One of the most widely accepted biblical understandings is that God does not change. There are many passages that attest to this (some are listed in the questions for group study at the end of this chapter). We will focus on the three most popular, but first we must tackle an unusual yet increasingly important word: *immutable*.

The term *immutable*, widely used in theological circles, comes from combining two ancient words. The Latin word *mutabilis* carries the meaning of *changeable*. When the Latin prefix *im-* is added, it negates the word that follows and elicits the meaning *not changeable* or *immutable*. Millard Erickson offers a concise definition: "Divine immutability . . . by this is meant that although everything else in the universe appears to undergo change, God does not. He is the unchanging eternal one."[8]

This definition may be lacking in precision. However, it is interesting to note that computer programmers use the terms mutable and immutable as well. In computer programming an immutable object is an object that cannot be modified once it is created; a mutable object is one that can be modified once it is fashioned.

Subsequently, because of an increasing use by software programmers and a continued use in theological circles, *immutable* is an increasingly helpful term for describing things that do not change.[9]

THREE BIBLICAL PASSAGES ON IMMUTABILITY

Many passages emphasize that God is unchanging (immutable), but three are cited with great frequency.[10] Let us look briefly at each, beginning with Psalm 102:1–3, 25–28.

Psalm 102:1–3, 25–28

Hear my prayer, O LORD;
>let my cry for help come to you.

Do not hide your face from me when I am in distress.
Turn your ear to me;
>when I call, answer me quickly.

For my days vanish like smoke;
>my bones burn like glowing embers.

In the beginning you laid the foundations of the earth,
>and the heavens are the work of your hands.

They will perish, but you remain;

> they will all wear out like a garment.

Like clothing you will change them and they will be discarded.

But you remain the same,

> and your years will never end.

The children of your servants will live in your presence;

> their descendants will be established before you.

A Verse-by-Verse Analysis. God's unchangeableness (vv. 25–28) is being extolled by a writer who is feeling rejected and in distress (vv. 1–3). Let us look at each of these verses.

Verses 1–2 Here we see the background for why the psalmist desires to be reminded of God's resilience and durability.

Verse 3 The writer is feeling as though he will not leave a legacy and that his "days vanish like smoke." He is feeling so afflicted and troubled that even his "bones burn like glowing embers."

Verse 25 In contrast to his impermanence, the writer emphasizes that the continuation of the "foundations of the earth" and "the heavens" are proof of God's permanence.[11]

Verse 26 Even though the seemingly permanent earth will one day pass away, God "will remain." The earth and heavens are temporary; like clothing they "will all wear out" and "like clothing you [God] will change them and they will be discarded." Thus God's eternalness and permanence is contrasted to even the temporariness of His creation.

Verse 27 The writer proclaims, "your years will never end," reminding us how different creation is from the Creator. Then the writer reiterates, "But you remain the same."

Verse 28 Finally, the writer notes that his ancestors will also live in God's presence. God is the writer's God, and He will also be the God of the writer's ancestors.

Thus, after a cry for permanence and resilience, the writer takes comfort in God's resilience and steadfastness. This gives the writer hope, for

God's love and presence will never fade. Jewish scholar Amos Hakham describes this contrast between God and His creation saying, "The Creator preceded His world, and will live long after it no longer exists. The Creator replaces His creations, like a person replacing his cloak."[12]

A Few Conclusions about God's Permanence. From this passage and the context the following conclusions may be drawn:

1. In His essential nature, God is eternal, permanent, and unlike His creation. He will not "wear out like a garment" (v. 26).
2. Thus, this passage reminds us that God endures and persists. His "years will never end" (v. 27), and future generations "will live in [his] presence" (v. 28). The emphasis in verses 26 and 27 is that God's permanence is different from His creation (He does not decay, waste away or become used up) and that He is eternal (He will be present in all generations).

We find here a passage extolling God's underlying permanence. The writer is seeking to assure his readers that "they need not be concerned as they see all that surrounds them deteriorating and changing. God is not like this. He is endless and ageless."[13] The emphasis is upon God's permanence and that He does not change in His essential nature, and this comforts the author of the psalm.

Malachi 3:6-12

"I the LORD do not change. So you, O descendants of Jacob, are not destroyed. Ever since the time of your forefathers you have turned away from my decrees and have not kept them. Return to me, and I will return to you," says the LORD Almighty.

"But you ask, 'How are we to return?'

"Will a man rob God? Yet you rob me.

"But you ask, 'How do we rob you?'

"In tithes and offerings. You are under a curse—the whole nation of you—because you are robbing me. Bring the whole tithe into the storehouse, that there may be food in my house. Test me in this," says the LORD Almighty, "and see if I will not throw open the floodgates of heaven and pour out so much blessing that you will not have room enough for it. I will prevent pests from devouring your crops, and the vines in your fields will not cast their fruit," says the LORD Almighty. "Then all the nations will call you blessed, for yours will be a delightful land," says the LORD Almighty.

A Verse-by-Verse Analysis. Verse 6. God begins His dialogue with a disobedient Jewish nation by reminding them in straightforward and robust language, "I the LORD do not change." Here He emphasizes that His essential nature has not changed, and He still expects the Jewish nation to abide by the essential nature of their commitments. This statement is in the perfect tense, a grammatical form that indicates something from the past is continuing through the present. This tense stresses "this truth as a fact of history but also as significant for the present. The Lord has not changed in the past and this is also applicable in the present time."[14]

Verse 7. This warning is necessary because the Jewish people have not been consistent in their nature by giving offerings and their tenth-portions (tithes). To this disobedience God decrees that they have left Him, and now they need to return. God anticipates their question: "How are we to return?" and addresses it in the next three verses.

Verse 8. Here God staunchly reminds them their refusal to bring tithes and offerings has made them robbers—robbers of God.

Verse 9. This results in a reciprocal action by God: He withholds His blessings from His people.

Verses 10–12. God calls them to "Test me in this . . . and see if I will not throw open the floodgates of heaven and pour out so much blessing that you will not have room enough for it." God does not reiterate the exact tithing procedures outlined in Leviticus 27:30–34 and Deuteronomy

14:22, for this Malachi passage is not about methodology, but about will and character. Thus, God draws attention to the underlying will and character qualities that are missing in the Jewish nation. God is calling the Jews to be unchanging in their essential nature and underlying convictions, as He is unchanging in these areas as well.

A Few Conclusions: Permanence in Nature, Will, and Character. This passage underscores the persistence and consistency of God's underlying nature, will, and character qualities—especially those of fairness, justice, love, and reciprocity.

In contrast, the Jewish nation's underlying qualities are depicted as not so persistent, nor pristine. Their underlying nature, will, and character are unreliable, fluctuating, and indecisive. This inconsistency is contrasted to God's magnificent consistency in nature, will, and character. Subsequently, a few lessons may be drawn:

1. Again, this passage is not about methodology, but rather about underlying nature, will, and character. This passage stresses that God does not change in nature, will, or character.
2. This persistence in God's qualities is contrasted with the lack of theses qualities in Jewish actions. These qualities are so neglected that the nation can be accused of robbery (vv. 8–9).
3. Therefore, this passage emphasizes underlying character qualities, and not methodologies. God finds no need to reiterate or reemphasize tithing and offering practices and structures that are outlined elsewhere.

From this passage we see a wonderful depiction of God's unchangeableness in nature, will, and character that includes fairness, justice, love, and reciprocity. In addition, His persistence in these qualities is contrasted with the Jewish nation's lack of persistency in these same attributes.

James 1:16-18

Don't be deceived, my dear brothers. Every good and perfect gift is from above, coming down from the Father of the heavenly lights, who does not change like shifting shadows. He chose to give us birth through the word of truth, that we might be a kind of firstfruits of all he created.

A Verse-by-Verse Analysis. Verse 16. James begins with an admonition so straightforward and strong that no one should entertain the thought that it could be untrue. "Don't be deceived" was a popular Greek attention-getting expression[15] that warned that to ignore the following would be a "serious moral failure."[16]

Verse 17. James follows with a powerful, poetic statement that God "does not change like shifting shadows." Here James emphasizes that God does not change in contrast to the unpredictable and fluctuating nature of shadows and silhouettes. The topic of this unchangeableness is God's desire to give good things to His children. James continues: "Every good and perfect gift is from above, coming down from the Father." James indicates he is not speaking about specific gifts, nor about God's methodology. Rather James is describing God's underlying and consistent nature as a giver. Again, this is not a passage about God's being unbendable in His methodology, but rather about His being unbendable in underlying nature.

Verse 18. This verse reconfirms that it is not method that matters, but rather God's unchanging *will* to give good gifts to His creation, His firstfruits. The term *firstfruits* refers to "the reborn, i.e., the Christians."[17]

A Few Conclusions. This passage is underscoring that God does not change in His underlying nature, will, and resultant character. Millard Erickson sums up: "These good gifts can be expected to continue to come and to be good, because the Father's character does not change at all."[18] Therefore, let's draw some conclusions.

1. God is unchangeable in His nature as a giver.

2. God is unchangeable in His will to give good gifts to His firstfruits.

3. As such, God exemplifies a Father (more on this in chapter 6), demonstrating consistent, persistent giving and generosity.

The physical actions of God's generosity and giving are not discussed; thus the conversation is not about method, but about God's consistency in character, especially that of giving.

From this and the other passages, we see recurring evidence that God's nature, will, and character are the focus, not His methodology.

THE BEGINNING OF A THEOLOGY OF CHANGE

God Is Unchangeable in Four Areas

Since God does not change in fundamental elements of His will or being, let us categorize His unchangeable characteristics into four areas.

God Is Unchangeable in His Permanence and Life. This means God does not change in His eternalness. God does not "wear out like a garment" (Ps. 102:26). The writer adds that though for humans our "days vanish like smoke . . . your [God's] years will never end" (Ps. 102:3, 27).

God Is Unchangeable in His Essential Nature of who He Is. This reminds us God does not change in His foundational, underlying nature of love, justice, compassion, giving, and grace. The psalmist summed this up by saying "you remain the same" (Ps. 102:27). And, God's inauguratory statement "I the LORD do not change" (Mal. 3:6) reminds the Jewish nation that God's essential nature does not change (even though those of the Jewish nation may). James' emphasis that God is a giver of "every good and perfect gift" (James 1:17) attests to His essential nature to be a giver and not a taker.

God's Will Is Unchangeable. God's purposes and desires, such as His desire to have fellowship with His creation and see all come to know Him, do not change. Again, God's desire to "give us birth through the word of truth, that we might be a kind of firstfruits of all he created" (James 1:18) attests to His will "to give," and to regenerate.

God Is Unchangeable in His Character. God's nature and will are exemplified in consistent and persistent character traits. Though God may exhibit character traits in different ways and manners, they are nonetheless consistent with His underlying nature and will. The three passages considered above carry many examples of God's unchangeableness in character, for example in "creating" (Ps. 102:25–26; James 1:18), in "blessing" (James 1:17–18; Mal. 3:10), in "reciprocating good for good" (Mal. 3:7, 10–12), in "fair dealing" (Mal. 3:7–9), as well "establishing," for the "children of your servants will live in your presence; their descendants will be established before you" (Ps. 102:28).

A COMPARISON OF GOD'S NATURE, WILL, AND CHARACTER

God's Nature (abbreviated examples[19])	God's Will (abbreviated examples)	God's Character (abbreviated examples)
Loving	God's will is that His people would know Him. • Matthew 28:18–20: "Then Jesus came to them and said, 'All authority in heaven and on earth has been given to me. Therefore go and make disciples of all nations, baptizing them in the name of the Father and of the Son and of the Holy Spirit, and teaching them to obey everything I have commanded you. And surely I am with you always, to the very end of the age.'" • 2 Peter 3:9b: "He is patient with you, not wanting anyone to perish, but everyone to come to repentance."	God seeks us and reaches out to us: • Luke 19:10: "For the Son of Man came to seek and to save what was lost." • John 4:23: "Yet a time is coming and has now come when the true worshipers will worship the Father in spirit and truth, for they are the kind of worshipers the Father seeks." • Revelation 3:20: "Here I am! I stand at the door and knock. If anyone hears my voice and opens the door, I will come in and eat with him, and he with me."
Just	God's will is to be separate from sin. • Romans 3:23: "For all have sinned and fall short of the glory of God." God judges us and proclaims there are none who are righteous. • Romans 3:10: "As it is written: 'There is no one righteous, not even one.'"	God punishes sin. • Romans 6:23a: "For the wages of sin is death . . ." • Exodus 32:33b: "Whoever has sinned against me I will blot out of my book." God blesses us when we do right. • Romans 6:23: "For the wages of sin is death, but the gift of God is eternal life

A COMPARISON OF GOD'S NATURE, WILL, AND CHARACTER

God's Nature (abbreviated examples)	God's Will (abbreviated examples)	God's Character (abbreviated examples)
Just	• Isaiah 53:6: "We all, like sheep, have gone astray, each of us has turned to his own way." God expects reciprocity. • Malachi 3:6–7: "'I the LORD do not change. So you, O descendants of Jacob, are not destroyed. Ever since the time of your forefathers you have turned away from my decrees and have not kept them. Return to me, and I will return to you,' says the LORD Almighty."	in Christ Jesus our Lord." • Malachi 3:7b: "'Return to me, and I will return to you,' says the LORD Almighty." • Romans 10:9: "That if you confess with your mouth, 'Jesus is Lord,' and believe in your heart that God raised him from the dead, you will be saved." God expects reciprocity. • 1 John 4:19: "We love because he first loved us." • Romans 12:1: "Therefore, I urge you, brothers, in view of God's mercy, to offer your bodies as living sacrifices, holy and pleasing to God—this is your spiritual act of worship." • 1 John 1:9: "If we confess our sins, he is faithful and just and will forgive us our sins and purify us from all unrighteousness."
Compassionate	God's will is to restore His people into fellowship with Him. • Zechariah 10:6: "I will strengthen the house of Judah and save the house of Joseph. I will restore them because I have compassion on them. They will be as though I had not rejected them, for I am the LORD their God and I will answer them." • Revelation 3:20: "Here I am! I stand at the door and knock. If anyone hears my	God cares for us. • 1 Peter 5:7: "Cast all your anxiety on him because he cares for you." God hurts for us. • Genesis 6:6: "The LORD was grieved that he had made man on the earth, and his heart was filled with pain." • Matthew 23:37: "O Jerusalem, Jerusalem, you who kill the prophets and stone those sent to you, how often I have longed to gather

A COMPARISON OF GOD'S NATURE, WILL, AND CHARACTER

God's Nature (abbreviated examples)	God's Will (abbreviated examples)	God's Character (abbreviated examples)
Compassionate	voice and opens the door, I will come in and eat with him, and he with me."	your children together, as a hen gathers her chicks under her wings, but you were not willing."
Love + Justice + Compassion = Salvation	God's will is to act himself, to restore us to fellowship with Him. • Philippians 2:5–8: "Your attitude should be the same as that of Christ Jesus: Who, being in very nature God, did not consider equality with God something to be grasped, but made himself nothing, taking the very nature of a servant, being made in human likeness. And being found in appearance as a man, he humbled himself and became obedient to death–even death on a cross!"	God sacrifices that which is most precious to Him to forgive our sins and restore our relationship to Him. • Romans 5:8: "But God demonstrates his own love for us in this: While we were still sinners, Christ died for us." • Romans 10:9–10: "That if you confess with your mouth, 'Jesus is Lord,' and believe in your heart that God raised him from the dead, you will be saved. For it is with your heart that you believe and are justified, and it is with your mouth that you confess and are saved." • Romans 10:13: "for, 'Everyone who calls on the name of the Lord will be saved.'"
Giving	God wants to give His creation "good gifts." • James 1:16–18: "Don't be deceived, my dear brothers. Every good and perfect gift is from above, coming down from the Father of the heavenly lights, who does not change like shifting shadows. He chose to give us birth through the word of truth, that we might be a kind of firstfruits of all he created."	God gave His Son, for our salvation. • John 3:16: "For God so loved the world that he gave his one and only Son, that whoever believes in him shall not perish but have eternal life." • Romans 8:32: "He who did not spare his own Son, but gave him up for us all—how will he not also, along with him, graciously give us all things?"

A COMPARISON OF GOD'S NATURE, WILL, AND CHARACTER

God's Nature (abbreviated examples)	God's Will (abbreviated examples)	God's Character (abbreviated examples)
Giving		God gave His Holy Spirit, for our empowerment. • Acts 5:32: "We are witnesses of these things, and so is the Holy Spirit, whom God has given to those who obey him." • Acts 15:8: "God, who knows the heart, showed that he accepted them by giving the Holy Spirit to them, just as he did to us." God gave His followers eternal life. • Romans 6:23a: "For the wages of sin is death, but the gift of God is eternal life in Christ Jesus our Lord." • Romans 8:1: "Therefore, there is now no condemnation for those who are in Christ Jesus."

To help the reader distinguish between nature, will, and character, the above is an abbreviated list of examples.

God Does Not Change in His . . . Permanence, Nature, Will, and Character. The above passages demonstrate a biblical theology of change must start with the understanding that God does not change in the internal aspects of His permanence, nature, will, and character.[20] This means He is unchanging in His underlying attributes.[21]

Thus, let us return to our list of strengths as perceived by church leaders:

1. Our church is a caring church.
2. Our church is a friendly church.
3. Our church emphasizes biblical teachings.

4. Our church leaders are hard working and care about the church.
5. Our church is where I find most of my friends.
6. Our church cares for families.
7. Our church cares for the needy.
8. Our church cares for all generations.
9. Our church cares for all people, regardless of culture.
10. Our church has a strong Sunday school program.
11. Our church has a strong youth program.
12. Our church has a strong children's ministry.
13. Our church has a good facility.
14. Our church has a strong music ministry.
15. Our church has a strong teaching ministry.

Note that leaders rated their top church strengths (1–9) as underlying and enduring attributes that resurface in a variety of different endeavors, ministries, and plans. Surveying church leaders reveals that what they value in a church is a steadfastness, permanence, and consistency in underlying character, nature and will.

Therefore we arrive at our first element in our biblical theology of change: *God does not change (is immutable) in His permanence, nature, will, and character.*[22] And, a secondary conclusion is that the Church as the body of Christ (1 Cor. 12:27) wants to mirror this, and should mirror it.

QUESTIONS FOR GROUP STUDY

1. Let each person look up a passage from one of the following categories. Then prepare a brief summary (an overview of less than 150 words) of that passage, explaining what it means for church leaders today.
   - **God is unchangeable in His *permanence* and *life*.**

Deuteronomy 32:39–40

Psalm 9:7–10

Psalm 55:16–19

Psalm 90:1–6

Psalm 102:12–17

Habakkuk 1:12

1 Timothy 1:15–17

1 Timothy 6:13–16

- **God is unchangeable in His essential *nature* of Who He is.**

Psalm 104:31–32

Romans 1:20

James 1:15–18

- **God's *will* is unchangeable.**

Job 23:13

Job 34:10–15

Psalm 33:10–12

Proverbs 19:21

- **God is unchangeable in His *character*.**

Exodus 34:6–7

Deuteronomy 4:29–31

Numbers 23:18–20

1 Samuel 15:27–29

Psalm 107:1–2

Isaiah 40:13–14

Lamentations 3:22–26

Micah 7:18–20

Romans 2:2

Romans 3:3–4

2 Timothy 2:11–13

Titus 1:2–3

2. Discuss the results. Then as a group, decide if there are

- reoccurring traits

- patterns that emerge
- other Scriptures that throw light on this subject

3. Make a list of God's unchangeable character qualities. Leave it open ended, to add more qualities as you discover and/or encounter them.
4. How does knowing God is immutable make you feel when going through trials or difficulties? Reread Psalm 102:11–28 in light of this question.

change reaction 5

what does the Bible say
about change?

the problem

some congregations realize
that change can be good but
are eager to ensure that they
remain faithful to the gospel.

when God changes

"That's the problem with Christians. You never change. You're stuck in old ways, always behind. Get with it!"

That phrase by a college roommate was my introduction to religious criticism. It occurred shortly after I had recommitted my life to Jesus in 1971. Growing up in a Christian home, I had only heard good things about Christianity and our church. But at a secular university, I encountered a different reaction.

To a certain extent that person was right. My roommate was unafraid to proclaim that he was opposed to organized religion, and he reminded me that culturally the church was often out of step.

Yet, our church had a robust youth and music ministry, and I found its leaders to be men and women of integrity and spirituality. In addition, they were contemporary in style, taste, and manner. But I also recalled the Amish Christians who lived nearby. They avoided modern conveniences. Yet, they did not live in biblical dress but in a culture reminiscent of the 1800s.

What was to be made of all this? Why was change so hard and inconsistent for Christians? Still, because no Christians lived in the dress and customs of New Testament times, some change had to be possible. Why was change so difficult? And why did Christians open themselves up to criticism on this subject?

Many years and much ministry later, I embarked on a church growth consulting practice. While I found it relatively easy to help churches see the potential for new ministries, I found it difficult for churches to actually change. There seemed an unseen force preventing churches from changing. Every time a church undertook the delicate subject, tension usually arose.[1]

It soon became evident that for church growth to occur and for the church to communicate its message in culturally relevant terms, some change is necessary. I began a twenty year investigation into church change, culminating in a D.Min. and a Ph.D. on this subject at Fuller Theological Seminary. In the process I found that change is a delicate force that can be wielded for good or bad. Part of this dilemma arises because Christians have a difficult time distinguishing when God changes and when He does not. So, we sometimes stumble in our application of change or ignore change in our churches for as long as possible.

While the previous chapter looked at what did *not* change about God (His permanence, nature, will, and character), in this chapter let's discover when God does change and in what ways.

When crafting a biblical theology of change, we must always begin with the Scriptures.

EIGHT TYPES OF BIBLICAL CHANGE

There are several types of change in the Bible.[2] I have codified them into a list of eight. I'll describe each and add a brief commentary.

- Type-1 change: **Change due to decline or deterioration.** This is the change we referred to in chapter 4 as change in permanence or life. There we saw that God does not change in His duration or eternalness. However, humans do undergo this type of change, for as the writer of Psalm 102:3 said, his "days vanish like smoke."
- Type-2 change: **Change in location.** Millard Erickson comments, "Since God presumably is not . . . spatially located, the sense of change as movement from one place to another does not apply."[3]
- Type-3 change: **Changes in quality.** When the Temple in Jerusalem replaced the makeshift Tabernacle, the Israelites experienced a positive change in the quality of the building in which they worshipped. (Compare Ex. 25 and 36 with 2 Chron. 3 and 4 for a description of the two buildings.) In a similar manner quality can lessen, for example when the Temple was rebuilt after the Babylonians destroyed it (see Ezra 3:12; Hag. 2:3). But changes in quality do not apply to God, for the Scriptures depict God as being all-powerful (Gen. 18:14; Job 42:2; Matt. 19:26) and thus having more power would be impossible.
- Type-4 change: **Change due to growth or improvement.** The Bible states that God is all good (Ex. 34:6; 1 Chron. 16:34) and thus improvement would be impossible.[4]
- Type-5 change: **Change of knowledge** means gaining knowledge that one did not possess before. Again, because God is all knowing (1 Sam. 2:3; 1 Chron. 28:9; John 16:30) additional or better knowledge is impossible.[5]
- Type-6 change: **Change in beliefs** "involves coming to hold different beliefs or attitudes."[6] We saw in chapter 4 that God is unchangeable in the essential *nature of who He is* (Ps. 102:27; Mal. 3:6; James

1:17) and that God's *will* is unchangeable (James 1:18). Thus God does not come to hold different beliefs or attitudes.

- Type-7 change: **Relational change** "involves not change in the thing itself, but in the relationship to another object or person."[7] This is an interesting thought. The biblical record tells us God *does* relate to us in different ways, depending on our reactions to Him. Note, God is not changing, but the relationship between Him and us does change. Thus, this type of change is found in the Bible.

- Type-8 change: **Change by taking different action than previously.** We see many times in the Bible where God takes a different action than He did previously. For example, when humans ask forgiveness, turn from their sins, and accept Jesus as their Savior, God takes different action (salvation, John 6:23; 10:9) than He had previously warned (damnation, Rom. 3:10, 23; 6:23; Rev. 21:8).[8]

Looking at the various types of change found in the Bible, it becomes clear that in most of these areas God does not change. Now, let's look at each of these types of change and see how they relate to God's unchangeableness in permanence, nature, will, and character.

GOD AND BIBLICAL CHANGE (TYPES 1–6)

Type 1

Because God is unchangeable in His permanence and life, He does not experience type-1 change: change due to deterioration.

We discovered that God is unchangeable in His *permanence* and *life* in chapter 4. We noted that this indicates that God does not change in His duration or eternalness. He does not "wear out like a garment" (Ps. 102:26), and though our "days vanish like smoke . . . [God's] years will never end" (Ps. 102:3, 27).

Therefore, type-1 change does not apply to God, for He does not decline nor deteriorate.

Types 2-5

Because God is unchangeable in His essential nature of who He is, God does not experience type-2, -3, -4, or -5 change.

The psalmist stated, "you remain the same" (Ps. 102:27), and God declared to a disobedient Israel lacking permanence in nature, "I the LORD do not change" (Mal. 3:6). Plus, James' emphasis that God is a giver of "every good and perfect gift" (James 1:17) reminds us it is God's essential nature to be a giver and not a taker.

God, by His nature, is present everywhere (Ps. 139:7–12), which means that God does not undergo change in location, type-2 change.

God's nature is all good (Ex. 34:6; 1 Chron. 16:34). This means He does not undergo type-3 change (change in quality) or type-4 change (growth improvement).

God's nature is all knowing (1 Sam. 2:3; 1 Chron. 28:9; John 16:30), meaning He cannot experience type-5 change (change in knowledge). How can someone who knows all, know more?

Type 6

Because God's will is unchangeable, God does not experience type-6 change—change in belief. We saw in chapter 4 that this means that God's purposes and desires, such as God's desire to "give us birth through the word of truth, that we might be a kind of firstfruits of all he created" (James 1:18), do not change.

Therefore, God's unchangeableness in His will means He does not experience type-6 change. His beliefs and attitudes are unchanging, and thus His will to act upon these beliefs also does not change.

Therefore, the first six types of change do not apply to God.

GOD AND TYPE-7 CHANGE (RELATIONAL)

That said, though, when we humans change our relationship to God (for example, instead of being estranged we ask forgiveness and return to Him), God does change the way He relates to us. Thus, a type-7 change, change in relationship, does occur. It is not God who is changing, He is remaining consistent to His underlying nature, will, and character. But, as He promised, the relationship between us and Him changes. We are no longer estranged, but restored to fellowship with Him (John 3:16; Rom. 8:32; 10:9–10; 1 John 1:9; Rev. 3:20).

In other words, because of the salvation brought about by Jesus Christ, we can be restored to fellowship with God. The relationship between us and God has undergone a change. As a result, God will not deal with us in a punitive manner. Romans 8:1 states, "Therefore, there is now no condemnation for those who are in Christ Jesus." The relationship has changed, but God has not changed, for He promised He would forgive us if we return to Him. What has changed is God's relationship to us, not God himself.

Let's look at a narrative that underscores this, The Parable of the Loving Father, and conduct a verse-by-verse analysis of Luke 15:11–32.

Jesus continued: "There was a man who had two sons. The younger one said to his father, 'Father, give me my share of the estate.' So he divided his property between them.

"Not long after that, the younger son got together all he had, set off for a distant country and there squandered his wealth in wild living. After he had spent everything, there was a severe famine in that whole country, and he began to be in need. So he went and hired himself out to a citizen of that country, who sent him to his fields to feed pigs. He longed to fill his stomach with the pods that the pigs were eating, but no one gave him anything.

"When he came to his senses, he said, 'How many of my father's hired men have food to spare, and here I am starving to death! I will set out and go back to my father and say to him: Father, I have sinned against heaven and against you. I am no longer worthy to be called your son; make me like one of your hired men.' So he got up and went to his father.

"But while he was still a long way off, his father saw him and was filled with compassion for him; he ran to his son, threw his arms around him and kissed him.

"The son said to him, 'Father, I have sinned against heaven and against you. I am no longer worthy to be called your son.'

"But the father said to his servants, 'Quick! Bring the best robe and put it on him. Put a ring on his finger and sandals on his feet. Bring the fattened calf and kill it. Let's have a feast and celebrate. For this son of mine was dead and is alive again; he was lost and is found.' So they began to celebrate.

"Meanwhile, the older son was in the field. When he came near the house, he heard music and dancing. So he called one of the servants and asked him what was going on. 'Your brother has come,' he replied, 'and your father has killed the fattened calf because he has him back safe and sound.'

"The older brother became angry and refused to go in. So his father went out and pleaded with him. But he answered his father, 'Look! All these years I've been slaving for you and never disobeyed your orders. Yet you never gave me even a young goat so I could celebrate with my friends. But when this son of yours who has squandered your property with prostitutes comes home, you kill the fattened calf for him!'

"'My son,' the father said, 'you are always with me, and everything I have is yours. But we had to celebrate and be glad, because this brother of yours was dead and is alive again; he was lost and is found.'"

Verse 11. When Jesus told this parable, there was a growing animosity between the religious people and the criminals (tax collectors) and sinners who were coming to Jesus (Luke 15:1–2). These criminals and outcasts were from a different culture than the religious people. The religious people began to mutter, "This man welcomes sinner and eats with them" (Luke 15:2). It was to address this cultural gulf between religious people and nonreligious people that Jesus gave five parables.

All five parables[9] are too expansive for us to address here, but the leader who wants to fully understand how relational change (type-7) occurs will want to study these passages. However, the purpose of all five parables was to help the religious leaders ("Pharisees and teachers of the law," Luke 15:2) understand that they needed to change their relationship with repentant sinners and lawbreakers. Each parable, including this one, reminds us that we must change our relationship with others if they demonstrate regret, seek forgiveness, and accept Jesus as the sacrifice for their sins.

Verses 13–16. The son was wrong in squandering "his wealth in wild living." And, his wayward living soon resulted in humiliation and calamity, for "He longed to fill his stomach with the pods that the pigs were eating, but no one gave him anything."

Verses 17–24. Recognizing his sin, the son declared, "I will set out and go back to my father and say to him: Father, I have sinned against heaven and against you." Now, a father's reaction could easily be "I told you so!" But the loving father of this parable, the fatherhood that Jesus wanted His hearers to emulate, ran passionately to welcome the wayward child home. Note the following points:

- Because the wayward son changed his attitude, the relationship changed. This is type-7 change. God demonstrates this when He forgives our sins, as we ask forgiveness and accept Jesus as our Savior. In addition, Jesus indicates in this parable that He expects His disciples to mirror this action of the loving father.

- The father takes the initiative to model and demonstrate the changed relationship.
- There is not an inkling of retribution or blame in the father's action.
- The father recognized the relationship had changed, and he celebrated rather than reprimanded.

Verses 28–30. The older brother felt slighted. He had been obedient and homebound. Jesus was insinuating that the older brother's reaction was similar to how religious people felt when they looked at the sinners and criminals coming to Jesus. The Pharisees and teachers of the law had been faithful, persistent, loyal, and trustworthy—just like the older brother.

Verses 31–32. Jesus told these persistent, loyal family members to rejoice that one who "was dead . . . is alive again; he was lost and is found." Jesus' message to address a growing rift between religious people and new converts was to emphasize that when sinners genuinely turn to Jesus, a new relationship occurs (type-7 change: relational change). We should expect and plan for such changes in relationships. And, we should celebrate them.

A Lesson for the Church. Though this parable is often called the parable of the prodigal son or parable of the lost son, it is really better designated the parable of the loving father. Here we see Jesus emphasizing how to behave when we are struggling with changes in relationship, especially between those who are returning to Christ. However, Jesus was not saying that all prodigals should be accepted. But, when the repentance and return is genuine as in this story, religious people (exemplified in the older brother) should mirror the actions of the father and celebrate a change in relationship.

As a church reaches out with the love of Jesus to people whose repentance is genuine, we must mirror the loving father's actions toward formerly estranged people. The same way the loving father ran to greet and celebrate with the remorseful prodigal, so must we be ready to forge a new relationship with those who return to Jesus.

Part of the problem today is that Christians forget (and I have succumbed to this as well) that we are not required to punish or shame those who genuinely return to Christ. It is tempting to say "I told you so." But our task is to disciple returnees in knowledge and nurture them—but not to condemn them. This begins by recognizing that a change in relationship has occurred.

Thus, we see type-7 change is a central part of the good news. Because the Holy Spirit is working on wayward lives (John 3:7–8), we must anticipate (and pray for) changes in relationships.

TYPE-8 CHANGE: TAKING DIFFERENT ACTION

Because of a change in relationships, God's action may be different than it was before. His permanence, nature, will, and character are not different, but His actions are. For example, when we ask God to forgive our sins, turn in a different direction, and believe Jesus has taken the penalty for our sins (Rom. 10:9–10), God forgives our wrongdoings (Rom. 5:8). But God had warned He would punish sin (Ezek. 18:4). It is not God's attitude that changed, but ours. In response God takes a different action than He had warned: one of restoration rather than retribution.

Millard Erickson explains, "God delivered the people of Israel from Pharaoh at one point in history, and sent His Son to the cross in another."[10] Let's look at several passages that illustrate how God takes different action.

God Takes Different Action Than Previously (Type-8 Change)		God's Unchanging Nature, Will, and Character
God saved Israel from Pharaoh (Ex. 6:2–8).	**God sacrificed** His Son (John 3:16).	• Loving • Compassionate • Forgiving
God in the old covenant instituted laws and regulations (Gen., Lev., etc.).	**God replaced the old covenant laws with a new covenant of grace** based on Jesus' sacrifice (Matt. 26:27–29) and our response of faith (Eph.	• God reaches out to His creation • God teaches His creation about himself. Galatians 3:24 states that the law was a tutor or

	2:8). The writer of Hebrews said "By calling this covenant 'new,' he has made the first one obsolete; and what is obsolete and aging will soon disappear" (Heb. 8:13).	schoolmaster to lead us to Christ. • God creates a new promise with His offspring (Heb. 9:15).
God commanded the circumcision of Abraham and his male descendents as a "sign of the covenant between me and you" (Gen. 17:10–11).	**The sign of God's covenant with His people became our faith in Him.** Paul summed this up, stating, "For in Christ Jesus neither circumcision nor uncircumcision has any value. The only thing that counts is faith expressing itself through love" (Gal. 5:6).	• God requires commitment. • God requires identification. • God requires faith. Faith must come from personal conviction.
Sacrificing animals in the Temple was required. Leviticus 1–7 itemizes the laws of sacrifices. However, David realized these rituals were meaningless if not done for the right reasons, writing about his own personal experience, "Sacrifice and offering you did not desire . . . burnt offerings and sin offerings you did not require" (Ps. 40:6). And, the prophet Samuel told Saul "to obey is better than sacrifice" (1 Sam. 15:22).	**Sacrificing animals in the Tabernacle/Temple is no longer required.** Jesus' sacrifice was a better sacrifice (Rom. 3:23–26) and took the place of ritualistic sacrifice (John 1:35–37). But, obedience and trusting that Jesus is our sacrifice and doing so for the right reasons is still needed (Rom. 3:28).	• God requires commitment. • God looks at the heart. • God reminds us we are unable to save ourselves. Jesus had to do this for us. When we accept His sacrifice and turn from our sins, Jesus becomes the sacrifice for us.
Unclean food was forbidden in Leviticus 11:1–23 and Deuteronomy 14:3–21 to ensure the Jewish people's health, to visibly distinguish them from other nations, and to avoid objectionable cultural associations (creatures that moved on the ground were associated with snakes, which often symbolized sin).[11]	**All food is clean**. Jesus "declared all food clean" in Mark 7:18–19. God also revealed this in a vision to Peter in Acts 10:9–16; 11:4–10.	• God can make any food clean. • The original rationale for food prohibitions was no longer required.

The Sabbath meant resting on the seventh day. A day of rest was one of God's commands to His people (Ex. 20:8). Violating this concept was forbidden (Num. 15:32–36).	**The Sabbath means resting, on any reoccurring day** (Mark 2:27–28). The idea of taking a day of rest is expected, but the exact day has become a personal conviction (Rom. 14:5–6).	• God wants a regular portion of our time. • God cares for His people and does not want them to go unconnected or unrefreshed.
Humankind was herbivorous (vegetarian). When God created the human race, they were initially herbivorous (Gen. 1:29).	**Humankind became omnivorous.** When conditions changed after the Flood, God commanded that His people also eat meat (Gen. 9:3), meaning they would be omnivorous. Norman Geisler said, "This change from herbivorous to omnivorous status is . . . not a contradiction . . . simply different commands for different people at different times in God's overall plan of redemption."[12]	• God adjusts His methodology with His people as circumstances and environments change. • But, God will never change in His nature to love, guide, and care for His creation.
In this lifetime we experience death (Rom. 5:12), **illness** (Matt. 10:1), **and tears** (Ps. 6:6), but also **miraculous signs** (Mark 16:17–18).[13]	**In heaven there will be no death** (1 Cor. 15:53–55), **illness** (Matt. 8:16–17), **tears** (Rev. 21:4), or need for **miraculous signs** (1 Cor. 13:8–12).	• God loves us. • God is preparing a better existence for us. • This better existence will be a change from what we experience in this world.

From the above and other passages we can see that God may change in methodology, but never in nature, will, or character. J. Rodman Williams sums this up, stating, "For example, God may seem to change from fearsome power to sacrificial love, but the seeming change is utterly dependable—He always and inevitably acts in uniform fashion. If, for example, man sins, he can expect God's punishment; if he repents, he can depend on God's forgiveness; if he seeks after God, he can count on God's presence: God changes not."[14]

The Repent Passages: When God *Repents*

Probably the most difficult passages in the Bible to tackle are those that say God *repents* of some action. The word *repent* carries the modern idea of having done something wrong with resultant regret and a plea for forgiveness. Contemporary dictionaries define *repent* as "regret, grieve for, or do penance for (a sin or crime)."[15] This definition certainly carries the idea of improper action, for which regret and forgiveness are needed. However, let us look at the passages in the Bible where *repent* is used to describe some action on God's behalf, and see if another perspective, a less contemporary and more biblical understanding, emerges.

> But Moses sought the favor of the LORD his God. "O LORD," he said, "why should your anger burn against your people, whom you brought out of Egypt with great power and a mighty hand? Why should the Egyptians say, 'It was with evil intent that he brought them out, to kill them in the mountains and to wipe them off the face of the earth'? Turn from your fierce anger; relent and do not bring disaster on your people" (Ex. 32:11–12).

Conclusions. The phrase "turn from your fierce anger; relent" (v. 12) is translated in the King James Version (KJV) "Turn from thy fierce wrath, and repent." Here confusion is created, because the KJV *repent* suggests the modern connotation of being sorry for a wrong action. However, the Hebrew word (*naham*) does not carry the thought of God being penitent or apologetic for some wrong action, but rather an anguish that leads to God changing His course of action, something an all-powerful God has the right to do. It is not error on God's behalf; it is a change in course. Erickson sums this up, saying, "Moses certainly seemed to think God capable of changing his commitment to a course of action."[16] Therefore, the New International Version translates *naham* more accurately as *relent*.

The LORD saw how great man's wickedness on the earth had become, and that every inclination of the thoughts of his heart was only evil all the time. The LORD was grieved that he had made man on the earth, and his heart was filled with pain. So the LORD said, "I will wipe mankind, whom I have created, from the face of the earth—men and animals, and creatures that move along the ground, and birds of the air—for I am grieved that I have made them" (Gen. 6:5–7).

Conclusions. Here again Erickson offers a helpful summation: "'The LORD was grieved that he had made man on the earth, and his heart was filled with pain.' . . . This appears to be a clear indication of God reversing his plan and doing what negates, at least with respect to some persons, his earlier life-giving endeavor."[17] In other words God, the giver of life, now grieves because of humankind's wickedness.

The King James Version translates verse 6 as "And it repented the LORD that he had made man on the earth, and it grieved him at his heart." This translation of *grieved* into *repent* (KJV) again confuses the meaning, suggesting God had been wrong in His previous actions. But this observation is only valid if we look at *repent* in the modern definition of "regret, grieve for, or do penance for (a sin or crime)."[18] The Hebrew word *naham* describes God's compassionate grief that leads to change in action (type-8 change), not a change in will, character, or nature.[19]

Not surprisingly, the New International Version (quoted above and throughout this book) carries more of the emphasis of the original Hebrew, that God was saddened over what His creation had become. This would be similar to the grief we could expect a loving father to feel over a wayward son (see Luke 15:11–32).

God responded, as He said He would, by being outraged by wickedness and ready to levy upon it the ultimate punishment: death. But because God's nature is grace and giving favor when favor is not due, God acted upon His nature and did not destroy humankind. The action is not in variance with His nature; it is consistent with it.

When God Repents

Richard Rice discusses God's repentance at length,[20] pointing out that God is not changing, for His actions are consistent with His underlying nature of love, justice, compassion, and giving. Rice's argument is that "the accounts of divine repentance are actually characteristic of God. He repents, not despite the fact that he is God, but because he is God. It is his very nature to repent, to relent of action he had planned to take, in light of human action and reaction."[21]

The point here is that part of God's nature is to relent upon an action, based upon humankind's responses. Thus, if we respond positively and appropriately, God does what He has promised and withholds His punishment. This would then be type-7 change, relational change, in addition to type-8 change, taking a different action than previously. And, thankfully for our eternal destiny, God demonstrates type-8 change too.

When Humans Repent

There are times in the Old Testament where *repent* refers to human regret (Ex. 13:17; Judg. 21:6) or our "humble agreement with God's righteous judgment" (Job 42:6; Jer. 31:19).[22]

And, human *repentance* in the New Testament (Greek *metanoeo*) carries both the ideas of human regret and genuine turning from one's sins (repentance). For example Judas *regretted* his betrayal of Jesus (Matt. 27:3), but it did not lead to a turning from his sins and a genuine repentance. Paul did not *regret* the sharp letter he wrote to the Corinthians (2 Cor. 7:8–10), because he hoped it would lead to their genuine turning from their sins (repentance).

Thus, we see that *repent* can be used to describe *regret* or *genuine repentance* among humans.[23] In addition, from the above discussion we can see that *repent* also can mean taking a different action than previously.

Thus, the result of our investigation is that repent is a more elastic word than customarily thought, with several definitions dependent upon context. Therefore to understand which meaning of *repent* is being used, we must, as we have done above, carefully investigate the biblical context of each usage.

WHAT DOES THIS MEAN FOR THE CHURCH?

Our Relational Change and God's Changing Actions

Even this short examination of Scripture alerts the reader to the fact that God changes in the way He deals with us depending upon how we react in our relationship to Him. When we repent, He remains consistent to His inner will (to have fellowship with us) and His underlying nature (to give forgiveness to those who seek genuine forgiveness). Examples of this abound.

And the Church as the body of Christ should reflect God's principles of change. Thus, we should be unchanging in nature, will, and character of love, forgiveness, compassion, service, and so forth. But, we also must be ready to change our actions based upon relational changes in unchurched people. In other words, when a person repents, we must mirror our Heavenly Father and forgive, embrace, celebrate, and edify.

Overcoming Cainotophobia—Change in Strategy Does Not Mean Change in Character

In similar fashion, we must understand that when we adjust our strategies to reach out to an unchurched culture with the good news, such change is not necessarily wrong if we (like God) remain true to a biblical and godly nature, will, and character.

The problem arises when we forget that change in our methodology can sometimes be good. We tend to wrongly label all change as bad—due to bad experiences with change in the past—in hopes of avoiding it. Subsequently, we forget about the eight types of biblical change. And, we fail to recall that while six types of biblical change may be inconsistent with God's character, God does experience relational change and taking a different action than previously.

Thus we must overcome any *cainotophobia*[24]—a fear of the results of change. God himself changes, albeit in consistent and holy ways.

Churches must be willing to change. But we must do so in consistent and holy ways. There is no room to let change deviate into sin, or to change in godly nature, will, or character. Rather, we must recognize that some types of change are warranted, as even God demonstrates. Therefore, we must carefully consider what should be changed—and what should *not* be changed.

THE TENSIONS OF CHANGE

Change is often ignored by Christians because it creates a tension and discomfort. Change forces us to look at what we are doing and evaluate it as to whether it is God-ordained or human-initiated. Change requires discussion, investigation, reflection, evaluation, and a solid biblical understanding. In our busy world today, we often fail to do this. We become stuck in our outdated ways of doing things, because change takes too much energy.

As a result, change is often overlooked until a crisis becomes so significant that it cannot be ignored. By then the change has polarized each side into competing camps, and discussion about biblical change is difficult.[25]

However, Christian scholars such as Jung Young Lee have pointed out that much of Christianity's discomfort with tension over change is not found in the Bible or in early Christianity. On the one hand, Lee points out that largely due to Greek thinking where everything was typically black or white, there crept into the Roman Church a non-biblical emphasis that everything was one way or the other. On the other hand, Lee points out that early Christians were influenced more by pre-Greek thinking, and they did not see any problem with God and His Church as changing in some regards and unchanging in others.[26]

Therefore, from the previous two chapters we should agree: a theology of biblical change must include both unchanging elements (as in God's nature, will, and character) and changing relationships and actions (as we see in God).

Let us look in chapter 6 at how an understanding of change might be modeled after the pattern of parenting, noting that the relationship of parent to child is one of the central allegories the Bible employs to explain God's relationship to humankind.

QUESTIONS FOR GROUP STUDY

1. Below are some additional verses about change. Use them, or go back to the table "God Takes Different Action Than Previously," to look at those passages in more detail.

   - Matthew 10:5–6
   - Mark 16:15
   - Luke 9:3
   - Luke 22:36

   Let these passages become discussion starters to help answer the following questions:

   - How does God view change?
   - Is all change good?
   - Is all change bad?
   - Is some change good? Give examples.
   - Is some change bad? Give examples.
   - How will you distinguish between when change is good, and when change is bad?

2. Cite other biblical examples in which God appears to change in His methodology.

3. Have you had to change your relationship with someone due to a change that person underwent? Has a person's asking you for forgiveness required you to relate differently to that individual? Or has a son or daughter matured and asked forgiveness with a result that you had to change the way you wanted to act toward him or her? Answer the following questions about how challenging it is when someone who is estranged asks to be forgiven.

   - What was your first reaction when the person asked forgiveness?
   - What did you do?
   - What do you wish you could have done?
   - What do you think the loving father from Luke 15:11–32 would have done?

4. God has boundaries He will not cross. As we saw in chapter 4, God will not change in His essential permanence, nature, will, or character. What are some of the essential areas you believe you cannot *and* should not change? List seven areas below:

1. _____

2. _____

3. _____

4. _____

5. _____

6. _____

7. _____

- Which of these changes are strictly personal preferences?
- Which of these changes reflect biblical boundaries?
- Discuss your answers with other leaders.

part three

UNCHANGING CHARACTER, CHANGING METHODS

the pattern
of parenting

In the two previous chapters we have come to the conclusion that underlying nature, will, and character must not change. But in tandem we see that certain relationships and actions do change. How we can best describe this duality will be our next topic of consideration.

Similarly, in chapter 1 we saw that church leaders, as well as congregants, are generally confused about the dual roles of a church, as a relational organization to be nurtured and as an administrative organization to be managed. This in another duality that requires careful balance.

As a parent of four daughters now in their twenties and thirties, I believe the pattern of parenting is one of the best models for balance amid such dualities.

Breanna always thought she had it the toughest. The eldest of four girls, Breanna was the child of our early twenties. Rebecca and I were joyful and anticipatory parents, launching into our duties with passion and zeal. Rebecca became a stay-at-home mom to spend time nurturing Breanna, while I worked ministerial jobs to support our fledging family.

We had good intentions. And as Christians who regularly participated in church life, we felt we had a biblical, moral, and altruistic perspective on parenting. We talked about how we wanted to share our Christian values and principles with our children—and Breanna was the guinea pig.

Today Breanna is a successful lawyer with her own growing family. Her hindsight vision has improved, as today she feels we did an excellent job in parenting her and often asks for advice. Little does she realize that in those early days, though we had principles and underlying standards, the parenting process was an experiment in how to live out those intentions in our fledgling family unit.

We learned as we went. With Breanna we had to improvise, adjust, and evaluate. She was the blessing of our life, as the Bible would say "the apple of our eye" (see Ps. 17:8). And though an enjoyable and pleasant journey, our task was filled with uncertainly as we balanced dualities of discipline and nurture and consistency and adaptation.

The end result was that Breanna felt we did a good job. But she also felt her younger sisters—Kelly, Corrie, and Ashley—had an easier time. The younger ones benefited from our experiences in living out our ideas with Breanna. Breanna was right: she did receive the lion's share of our improvisation, changeableness, adaptations, and experimentation. Yet, with each daughter, Rebecca and I learned how to better inculcate our principles into our parenting actions.

What helped us succeed in raising four happy daughters was that we adjusted our actions as our daughters matured. We never adjusted our underlying belief systems or principles. But, we found varying and more effective ways to live out our principles in our parenting actions.

What was happening was that as the girls matured, our relationship changed (a type-7 change). As a result, we had to take different action than previously (type-8 change). In hindsight, it was our ability to be consistent in nature, will, and character in the face of four children undergoing different stages of childhood development. Our parenting actions were different when our daughters were preschoolers than when they were teenagers. But we were careful to ensure they knew our nature, will, and character remained the same.

Today, though we miss the marvelous escapades of our youthful brood, Rebecca and I relate to our daughters as adults. Our relationships with them have changed as they matured. As a result, our parenting actions had to adjust.

Shortly before the birth of her first child, Breanna inquired about our parenting skills. "We were children, too," replied Rebecca. "But we had underlying biblical principles, and we sought to continually be a better and better example of Christian parenting—but it took a lot of learning and adjustment." Breanna smiled and said no more about the topic. She understood this better than Rebecca or I.

GOD'S PATTERN OF PARENTING

The Bible is rife with the pattern of parenting as reflected in God's relationship to His offspring. Let's look at a few examples of God's parenting principles and see what lessons they can engender for leaders tackling church change.

God as Mother

The Scriptures describe God as having the best attributes of *both* father and mother. Since the attributes of a mother are often the most overlooked, let's begin our inquiry with several motherly attributes of God.

God Has an Enduring Motherly Relationship. "Can a mother forget the baby at her breast and have no compassion on the child she has borne? Though she may forget, I will not forget you!" (Isa. 49:15).

God Comforts, as a Mother Comforts a Child. "As a mother comforts her child, so will I comfort you" (Isa. 66:13).

God Yearns Like a Woman in Childbirth. God longs for the growth and maturity of His people. Isaiah 42:14–15 says, "For a long time I have kept silent, I have been quiet and held myself back. But now, like a woman in childbirth, I cry out, I gasp and pant. I will lay waste the mountains and hills and dry up all their vegetation; I will turn rivers into islands and dry up the pools." Also, James 1:18 reads, "He chose to give us birth through the word of truth, that we might be a kind of firstfruits of all he created."[1]

God Longs to Protect and Nurture Resistant Offspring. In Matthew 23:37 Jesus used the imagery of a mother hen and her chicks, avowing, "O Jerusalem, Jerusalem, you who kill the prophets and stone those sent to you, how often I have longed to gather your children together, as a hen gathers her chicks under her wings, but you were not willing."

God as Father

Here Scripture passages abound.[2] The following are a few examples. Many more verses will be discussed in the following section, "God as Parent."

God Loves Us as a Father Loves His Children. First John 3:1 says, "How great is the love the Father has lavished on us, that we should be called the children of God! And that is what we are!"

God Is "Abba, Father." One of the most remarkable New Testament passages is Romans 8:15: "For you did not receive a spirit that makes you a slave again to fear, but you received the Spirit of sonship. And by him we cry, 'Abba, Father.'" Another is Galatians 4:6: "Because you are sons, God sent the Spirit of his Son into our hearts, the Spirit who calls out, 'Abba, Father.'" See also how Jesus used the expression "Abba" when referring to His Heavenly Father in Mark 14:36.[3] The term *abba* is an Aramaic expression of endearment and familiarity customarily used by a young child.[4] It is usually the first word from a child's mouth. While some translate this *daddy,* this may still be too formal. A better term might be *dada,* an expression connoting dependence, endearment, commencement, and closeness. This intimate, reliant, and cherished term gives new insight to how God longs for us to return to Him and recapture that early father-child connection and love.

God Must Discipline Us at Times, as a Loving Father. Solomon warned in Proverbs 3:11–12, "My son, do not despise the LORD's discipline and do not resent his rebuke, because the LORD disciplines those he loves, as a father the son he delights in." Also, Hebrews 12:9–10 states, "Moreover, we have all had human fathers who disciplined us and we respected them for it. How much more should we submit to the Father of our spirits and live! Our fathers disciplined us for a little while as they thought best; but God disciplines us for our good, that we may share in his holiness."

Alister McGrath said, "to speak of God as father is to say that the role of the father in ancient Israel allows us insights into the nature of God."[5] Thus, we can catch a glimpse into God's loving, preserving, just, and devoted nature.

God as Father and Mother

Sometimes God appears in the role of both parents. For example, in Psalm 27:10 we see, "Though my father and mother forsake me, the LORD will receive me."

Moses' song of adoration (Deut. 32) characterized God's love toward His children as that of a paternal eagle, hovering over its young and protecting them. The tasks outlined—hovering over the young, catching them, and carrying them—describes female eagle attributes, but also can describe male eagles. Thus, both roles can be inferred. The full passage reads, "In a desert land he found him, in a barren and howling waste. He shielded him and cared for him; he guarded him as the apple of his eye, like an eagle that stirs up its nest and hovers over its young, that spreads its wings to catch them and carries them on its pinions" (Deut. 32:10–11).

Deuteronomy 32:18 describes both maternal and paternal roles of God in the same sentence: "You deserted the Rock, who fathered you; you forgot the God who gave you birth."

Sallie McFaque gives a helpful summation of God as father and mother: "God as mother does not mean that God is mother (or father). We imagine God as both mother and father, but we realize how inadequate these and any other metaphors are to express the creative love of God . . . . Nevertheless, we speak of this love in language that is familiar and dear to us, the language of mothers and fathers who give us life, from whose bodies we come, and upon whose care we depend."[6]

God's parental love is so deep, it is almost unfathomable in magnitude, scale, and reach. There is little surprise that both motherhood and fatherhood expressions are needed to describe such love. Ephesians 3:17–19 puts it this way: "And I pray that you, being rooted and established in love, may have power, together with all the saints, to grasp how wide and long and high and deep is the love of Christ, and to know this love that surpasses knowledge—that you may be filled to the measure of all the fullness of God."

Fatherhood certainly occurs with more frequency in biblical passages. This may be due to the patriarchal culture of ancient times.[7] However, that in such patriarchal times the writers of the Scriptures would not flinch at describing God's motherly attributes indicates God has no opposition to using the best attributes of fatherhood *and* motherhood to describe His character.

Fatherhood and motherhood can be defined in various ways depending upon the relationship. For example, fatherhood can describe the establishing of a household; the headship of that household; and the provision, care, and feeding of that household. As we saw above, motherhood can describe birthing, nurturing, cherishing, and more.

However, to keep this study from becoming too lengthy, let us look at how the fatherhood and motherhood of God relates to parenting. In the process, let's discover some strategic guidelines for dealing with change in churches.

God as Parent

Loves. "How great is the love the Father has lavished on us, that we should be called the children of God! And that is what we are!"[8] (1 John 3:1).

Nurtures. "Because you are sons, God sent the Spirit of his Son into our hearts, the Spirit who calls out, 'Abba, Father'" (Gal. 4:6).

Sustains. "Therefore I tell you, do not worry about your life, what you will eat or drink; or about your body, what you will wear. Is not life more important than food, and the body more important than clothes? Look at the birds of the air; they do not sow or reap or store away in barns, and yet your heavenly Father feeds them. Are you not much more valuable than they? Who of you by worrying can add a single hour to his life?" (Matt. 6:25–27).

Teaches. "Jesus replied, 'If anyone loves me, he will obey my teaching. My Father will love him, and we will come to him and make our home with him. He who does not love me will not obey my teaching. These words you hear are not my own; they belong to the Father who sent me . . . . But the Counselor, the Holy Spirit, whom the Father will send in my name, will teach you all things and will remind you of everything I have said to you" (John 14:23–26).

"Anyone who runs ahead and does not continue in the teaching of Christ does not have God; whoever continues in the teaching has both the Father and the Son" (2 John 9).

John Miller states, "God himself is characterized as just such a compassionate teaching father in Hosea's portrait of the way, when Israel was an infant, he chose him, fed him, embraced him, taught him to walk, and, as Israel grew older, instructed him 'with leading strings of love'" (Hosea 11:1–4).[9]

Gives. "If you, then, though you are evil, know how to give good gifts to your children, how much more will your Father in heaven give good gifts to those who ask him!" (Matt. 7:11). "Do not be afraid, little flock, for your Father has been pleased to give you the kingdom" (Luke 12:32). "I keep asking that the God of our Lord Jesus Christ, the glorious Father, may give you the Spirit of wisdom and revelation, so that you may know him better" (Eph. 1:17).

Loses. "You deserted the Rock, who fathered you; you forgot the God who gave you birth" (Deut. 32:18, again maternal and paternal roles described in the same sentence).

Grieves. "O Jerusalem, Jerusalem, you who kill the prophets and stone those sent to you, how often I have longed to gather your children together, as a hen gathers her chicks under her wings, but you were not willing" (Matt. 23:37).

Comforts. "As a mother comforts her child, so will I comfort you" (Isa. 66:13). "You have heard that it was said, 'Love your neighbor and hate your enemy.' But I tell you: Love your enemies and pray for those who persecute you, that you may be sons of your Father in heaven. He causes his sun to rise on the evil and the good, and sends rain on the righteous and the unrighteous" (Matt. 5:43–45).

Casts out fear. "For you did not receive a spirit that makes you a slave again to fear, but you received the Spirit of sonship. And by him we cry, 'Abba, Father'" (Rom. 8:15).

Disciplines. "My son, do not despise the LORD's discipline and do not resent his rebuke, because the LORD disciplines those he loves, as a father the son he delights in" (Prov. 3:11–12). "Endure hardship as discipline; God is treating you as sons. For what son is not disciplined by his father?" (Heb. 12:7).

And Hebrews 12:9–10: "Moreover, we have all had human fathers who disciplined us and we respected them for it. How much more should we submit to the Father of our spirits and live! Our fathers disciplined us for a little while as they thought best; but God disciplines us for our good, that we may share in his holiness."

Protects. "In a desert land he found him, in a barren and howling waste. He shielded him and cared for him; he guarded him as the apple of his eye, like an eagle that stirs up its nest and hovers over its young, that spreads its wings to catch them and carries them on its pinions" (Deut. 32:10–11).

Sacrifices. "For God so loved the world that he gave his one and only Son, that whoever believes in him shall not perish but have eternal life" (John 3:16).

Has Compassion. "Can a mother forget the baby at her breast and have no compassion on the child she has borne? Though she may forget, I will not forget you!" (Isa. 49:15). "But while he was still a long way off, his father saw him and was filled with compassion for him; he ran to his son, threw his arms around him and kissed him" (Luke 15:20).

Reaches Out. "O Jerusalem, Jerusalem, you who kill the prophets and stone those sent to you, how often I have longed to gather your children together, as a hen gathers her chicks under her wings, but you were not willing." (Matt. 23:37). "When Israel was a child, I loved him, and out of Egypt I called my son. But the more I called Israel, the further they went from me" (Hos. 11:1–2).

Forgives. "For if you forgive men when they sin against you, your heavenly Father will also forgive you" (Matt. 6:14). "But love your enemies, do good to them, and lend to them without expecting to get anything back. Then your reward will be great, and you will be sons of the Most High, because he is kind to the ungrateful and wicked. Be merciful, just as your Father is merciful" (Luke 6:35–36).

Restores and Gives Life. "Yet to all who received him, to those who believed in his name, he gave the right to become children of God—children born not of natural descent, nor of human decision or a husband's will, but born of God" (John 1:12–13). "For just as the Father raises the dead and gives them life, even so the Son gives life to whom he is pleased to give it" (John 5:21).

Continues. Once a parent, you are always a parent, regardless of estrangements that may come. There is always a link that, though severed legally, emotionally, or by physical distance, still resides somewhere deep within our psyche. Isaiah 49:15 says, "Can a mother forget the baby at her breast and have no compassion on the child she has borne? Though she may forget, I will not forget you!" After studying the history of the early church, Peter Widdicombe noted that parenthood is a "relational continuity caused by a free act of God's will."[10] In other words, a key attribute of God's parenthood is the commitment that parenthood fosters.

Consistent in Nature, Will, and Character. In all God's parenting endeavors, He remains consistent to His underlying nature, will, and character as loving, just, gracious, caring, merciful, and holy.

Howard Marshall succinctly sums up God's parenting, noting, "For disciples of Jesus, as for Jesus, God is experienced as a loving Father who cares for his children and with whom they have an intimate personal relationship expressed in prayer."[11]

Now, let us see if we can extract from these patterns of parenting guidelines for change that can help a church stay true to its underlying principles while adapting to changing environments, ages, and circumstances.

APPLICATIONS FOR CHANGE FROM THE PATTERN OF PARENTING

Application 1: Never Waiver in Your Underlying Principles

Herein lies a key to successful parenting. Children are experts in noting duplicity and deceit. They flourish with consistency and reliability. Here then are two points for maintaining underlying principles:

- Use your principles to create boundaries you will not cross and you will not allow your offspring to cross.
- State these boundaries to help you remember and keep from wavering in those underlying qualities (we will do this in an eight-stage process in chapter 7).

Application 2: While Remaining Within Your Boundaries, Use the Pattern of Parenting to Adjust Your Actions

As children grow, different actions must accompany the changing relationship between parent and child. Every parent soon realizes actions that worked with preadolescent children will not work with teens. Life quickly teaches that actions that worked with teens will not be effective when the offspring are adults.

Changes in actions (type 8) are required by the following changes in relationships (type 7):

- **Relational changes due to the stage of life (child, adolescent, etc.):**
  Parenting Actions: Child psychologists such as Jean Piaget and Erick Erickson discovered that children develop through various stages of understanding. Parenting tools that work at one stage may not work at another.
  Church Actions: Churches also go through different stages of life. A newly started church may look to the pastor as the expert to lead the way, while a church with a long history may have a cadre of mature leaders with whom the pastor must partner.

- **Relational changes due to the environment (college, friends, neighbors, etc.):**
  Parenting Actions: When our children left home for college, we trusted the principles we had instilled in them as youth would guide them. With difficulty Rebecca and I trusted our daughters to make good choices. Though there were daily times we wished to pick up the phone and check up on them, prayer became the preferred avenue for influence.
  Church Actions: Today, younger generations have different music, language, stories, styles, and outlook than their parents. As such, once we have effectively discipled young people, we must trust them to sift elements of culture, filtering out the bad and retaining the godly. It is often difficult from our perch in another culture to

refrain from offering our opinion or advice. Again, like a college daughter or son, our primary influence is in what we have taught and modeled, and in continuing prayer.

- **Relational changes due to individual changes (marriage):**
  Parenting Actions: As our children married, our relationship changed further, and for the better. We related as adults, but differently. Sometimes the paternal instinct would arise with such ferocity that containing it was challenging. But in marriage our offspring now have new responsibilities and relationships.
  Church Actions: Churches often undergo internal change as congregations age or balances of ethnicity shift. New networks emerge, in much the same way as a marriage welcomes in a new extended family into our erstwhile comfort. New actions in almost every area of life are required.

Application 3: Carefully, Biblically, and Regularly Evaluate Your Boundaries

Boundaries are artificial lines in the sand that help us stay true to our underlying nature, will, and character. Not all boundaries are principles. While godly nature, will, and character should not change, boundaries may change. The way we live out those principles in our parenting and in our change process may need to be adjusted based on further knowledge. While this does not apply to God because He knows all and is all good, this does apply to us, His fallible creatures. Thus, unlike God we must be ready to reevaluate our boundaries to ensure they truly reflect our underlying principles and have not been inadvertently created by our cultural, generational preferences or biases. Chapter 7 will look at steps to evaluate our statements of change boundaries.

Assessment and appraisal are designed to ensure that our boundaries reflect our underlying nature, will, and character. This is not to suggest that underlying principles change, but rather a reminder that boundaries do.

Application 4: Move Forward Humbly, Slowly, and with Copious Amounts of Prayer and Bible Study

Parenting Actions. Rebecca and I found ourselves encountering unforeseen difficulties in parenting. Often unexpectedly we were thrust into situations we had no idea we might encounter. What rescued us from these conundrums was a guiding biblical nature, will, and character. Often Rebecca and I would have to stop and pour over the Bible to ascertain if the problem was addressed by Scripture. If it was not directly addressed in the Word, copious amounts of prayer and advice from godly friends became the requisite avenue.

Church Actions. Churches encounter change with both the unknown and the unexpected. With new cultures come new ideas. With new generations come new artistic forms. With maturing Christians, much like maturing children, come new expectations, delegation opportunities, and heightened levels of trust. Much like missionaries, Christians must sift through a culture and see which elements are appropriate and which go against the teachings of Jesus.

THE POWER OF PARENTING

"I need a break" is a change reaction we often hear congregants lament. As parents we may feel this way too. But the pattern of parenting is that we persist—because we must. As parents, we rely on foundational principles while adjusting actions—because it works.

Jesus acknowledged that His empowerment and patterns were based on what He observed His Heavenly Father doing. Thus John 5:19 states, "Jesus gave them this answer: 'I tell you the truth, the Son can do nothing by himself; he can do only what he sees his Father doing, because whatever the Father does the Son also does.'"

Herein lies a good example for Jesus' followers. In the parenting patterns of God we see a remarkable, extensive, organic, connected relationship that helps us in our journey of discipleship. We see that an integral part of the pattern of parenting is to remain steadfast in boundaries based on nature, will, and character. At the same time it is important to remain elastic in actions due to changing relationships.

Thus, the chapter 7 will look at how a church can craft a Statement of Change Boundaries (SCB) that will help the congregation decide which changes are appropriate and which changes go too far.

QUESTIONS FOR GROUP STUDY

Have each leader choose from one of the options below, and bring the completed question to your leadership meeting. Have each leader share his or her response without comment by other leaders. After everyone has had a opportunity to share, open the discussion for general or specific comments.

1. Give two examples of how your parenting style changed as your children matured.
2. Describe different stages you've witnessed your children going through.
3. Explain the three biggest adjustments you had to make in your parenting actions (in actions, not nature, will, or character).
4. Tell your biggest blunder as a parent.
5. Tell your greatest success as a parent.
6. Give two examples of how churches undergo change in stages of life, in their community context, or in their congregational makeup.
   * Have these changes been for the worse?
   * Have these changes been for the better?
7. Give three examples of how your church leadership style has changed for different situations.
8. Pick two of the following Scripture verses, and tell how they can help you become a more effective leader.
   Numbers 11:12
   Deuteronomy 32:10

Deuteronomy 32:18
Psalm 27:10
Psalm 17:8
Psalm 90:2
Isaiah 42:14
Isaiah 49:15
Isaiah 66:12
Isaiah 66:13
Matthew 7:11
Matthew 23:37
Romans 8:15
Galatians 4:6
Ephesians 3:17
James 1:18

how to create statements of change boundaries

My father, Gerald, was a carpenter at heart. Though he earned his living owning an appliance store, he yearned to return to his boyhood craft of woodwork. In our living room stands a bookshelf designed and crafted by Gerald when he was a teen in the 1930s. Though Dad never returned to his boyhood trade, carpentry euphemisms regularly peppered his observations.

"You're long on talk and short on action," was one of those favorite sayings. This comment often accompanied some task to which I was appointed, but which I liked to ruminate about more than tackle. To me, part of the enjoyment of every action, every task, was to ponder, investigate, and verbally brainstorm. Subsequently, I rarely got to the conclusion of any project. The process was so enjoyable for an investigative person as myself, that the longer my exploration and musings lasted, the happier I remained. Finishing a task meant the end of an enjoyable reflective process. I guess this is what led me into academia.

My love for analysis and disdain for completion was driven out of me once I entered ministry. I soon learned that to reach people for Christ I had to wed my enjoyment of the process with a goal orientation. Graduate school similarly codified in me the importance of deadlines and goals, and today I enjoy the conclusion as much as the journey.

But, it was not always so. My father was often frustrated as I eschewed the goal and enjoyed the ride. When I did so, "Long on talk and short on action" was Dad's customary observation. He never uttered it in a vindictive manner or in an unsympathetic voice. Rather it was delivered with the sigh of a parent who wishes to make his point without exasperating his child. My father was a man of God, and in this and many other actions he mirrored Ephesians 6:4: "Fathers, do not exasperate your children; instead, bring them up in the training and instruction of the Lord."

After years of church growth consulting, I have noted that churches often reflect my youthful personality. Churches can spend months, perhaps even years, debating the strengths and weaknesses of some endeavor, all the while sacrificing the immediacy and effectiveness of a conclusion. Long on talk and short on action.

One client began discussing adding a modern worship celebration[1] in 1990. Though the modern worship movement could be traced back to the 1960s, this church began considering the topic almost three decades later. Nonetheless, a desire among baby boomers in the church for a modern worship expression led church leaders to begin discussing it. In heated meetings, some I attended but even more I avoided, congregational leaders in both the administrative council and worship committee debated worship pros and cons. Over a decade later (2001) they launched a modern worship service. Within two years, attendance grew 34 percent. The pent-up demand was being met, and the modern service grew larger than the traditional service. Congregants were now delighted that they had added a modern worship option.

As we will note in chapter 8, it is important to move cautiously building consensus before any major change is implemented. However, a decade for this church's decision was a bit drawn out. This fact was brought home when I encountered a former church leader soon after the church's growth. I inquired about how he felt now that the modern worship service he had longed for was a reality. "We don't go to First Church anymore," came his reply. "In the mid-nineties many of us left to go to Hometown Community Church. I guess for the sake of our families we couldn't wait any longer." I knew Hometown Community Church; its pastor was a friend who regularly solicited my advice. And now Hometown Community Church was a megachurch, with nearly two thousand people in Sunday attendance. This church had tapped into a need in the area, offering from its inception a myriad of modern worship celebrations each Sunday.

The story is not a travesty, for many community residents today are worshipping in both modern and traditional expressions. What is disheartening, is that there are many people who could have been reached over those ten years by both churches if they had both offered modern and traditional worship options instead of one or the other.

The fault mirrors the same weakness I exhibited to my dad. "Long on talk and short on action" is often what results when we consider change. One of this book's goals is to prevent this from happening.

To thwart this tendency, this chapter will deal with eight steps churches can undertake to ensure that they do not just talk about change, but actually do it. We will commence by creating mutually agreed-upon boundaries in which our change must fit. This chapter is one of the most important in the book, for it will move us forward and ensure we are not only "long on talk" but also "persistent in action."

STATEMENTS OF CHANGE BOUNDARIES

To this point, we have described the Statement of Change Boundaries (SCB) from varying perspectives. Now it is time to tender a definition: The SCB depicts the limits, borders, and boundaries of principles and actions across which congregants mutually agree that change should not cross. This exercise is critical for allying fears of reticent congregants, as well as ensuring change does not fundamentally alter a church's nature, will, or character.

Not only principles are listed, but also examples of actions that cross congregational boundaries. Thus, an SCB has the following characteristics:

1. Some parts of the statement are evolving, and some are not.
   - Not changing: *Principles* of the church (i.e., nature, will, and character) and theology should not change.
   - Changing: *Actions* will change due to changes in relationships (type-7 change) or because different action is warranted (type-8 change).
2. The SCB is regularly reviewed before any major change is implemented to ensure changes do not cross predefined boundaries.
3. The SCB is published regularly to help define the character, personality, and direction of the congregation.
4. The SCB is less than one page, single-spaced (350 words per page), with one additional page (again 350 words) of examples.
5. The SCB is consulted whenever a potentially divisive change is considered. In such circumstances, the following action is taken:
   - The change is seen to be consistent with the SCB.
   - Or if the change crosses a boundary of the SCB the following is undertaken:
     - Discussion is opened to consider changes in the SCB. (This would follow the format outlined later in this chapter under step 6.)

○ If the change is deemed beyond the boundaries the congregation has adopted, the change is not implemented.

EIGHT STEPS TO CREATING A STATEMENT OF CHANGE BOUNDARIES

Step 1: Do Your Homework

Denominational Theology and Traditions. Churches have personalities and theologies based upon denominational and local histories, perspectives and convictions. To craft an SCB first requires a consultation of the denominational statement of faith. These are the basic values that undergird the network of churches to which a congregation may belong.[2] Reading and understanding each of the points in a statement of faith is a critical beginning for understanding boundaries.

For example, a non-instrumental Church of Christ may want to ensure that musical boundaries include the denominational preference for non-instrumental worship. In these congregations worship is conducted by voices only, without musical accompaniment. This is an important distinctive for churches of this denomination, and they may wish to include a statement in their SCB that changes in worship will not cross the non-instrumental boundary into instrumental forms.

In addition, there is little that could prevent a non-instrumental congregation from having modern worship or even postmodern worship with voice accompaniment only. I have witnessed many youthful organic congregations engaged in compelling worship services where instruments were eschewed in lieu of *a cappella* praise.

Unique Characteristics of Your Congregation. Each congregation has unique giftings[3] that should be reflected in its SCB.[4] Here are some examples of unique characteristics that can be found in individual congregations:

• Some are uniquely gifted in music.
• Others are noted for the oratory of their speakers and teachers.

- Churches may have a unique emphasis on supporting missionaries and mission programs.
- Other congregations may have a multigenerational, multiracial, or multiethnic composition.
- Often churches are known for the ministries they provide for the community:
  thrift shop
  food pantry
  twelve-step program
  support for a specific program, such as Habitat for Humanity, United Way, special educational, etc.
  teen ministry
  daycare program
  preschool
- Churches may be known for ministries they provide for the community *and* congregation, such as:
  ministry to youth
  choir
  women's ministry
  men's ministry
  young adult ministry
  small groups
  Sunday school classes
  primary or secondary school

For example, a church that has an active Stephen Ministry program will want to ensure this is reflected in their change boundaries. Stephen Ministry[5] is a training program that empowers and trains volunteers within the congregation to "provide one-to-one Christian care to hurting people in and around your congregation."[6] This valued and effective program should be reflected in the SCB.

If a program like Stephen Ministries was not reflected in the SCB, conflict and clashes could erupt over new ideas. For example, in a church with a vibrant Stephen Ministry, a change in charter to require that all hospital visitation be conducted by ordained clergy might cross a boundary stating, "We will do nothing that undermines, weakens or destabilizes our church's Stephen Ministry." Stephen Ministers are often involved in hospital visitation, and taking away this duty would undercut the program. When support of the Stephen Ministry is reflected in an SCB, conflicting ideas become less divisive, for those pushing for change can see it goes against one of the unique characteristics of this congregation. It has been my experience that SCBs help communicate throughout a congregation those things that the church feels are important. As a result, changes that undermine a unique congregational focus are usually not pursued.

A final example might help. A client church felt its choir, though now decimated by old age, was still a viable strength of the congregation. The community knew of this church primarily because of its gifted choir, even though they were waning in numbers. Thus the choir leader, whose first name was Varner, was an icon in the area. He had led choir camps for years at a nearby religious retreat center, and he had led dozens of adult choir tours to Europe. To the community and to this church, the choir director and the choir were a core competency.

A new pastor was assigned to this congregation, and he set out to attract the many baby boomers who lived in this area. Since there was only one Sunday worship service, and the choir took up a good portion of that service, the pastor decided the choir should be replaced by a modern worship team. "The choir numbers only eighteen people," the pastor recalled. "And, people have been asking for contemporary music for years." Against my advice, the pastor ended the choir and replaced it with a worship team. The choir leader took me aside at my next visit and complained about the introduction of what he called "radio music." Akin to music he heard (only in fleeting moments) on the radio, Varner was aghast that the pastor would replace an important choir program with radio refrains. Also aghast were the choir, the community, and congregants who enjoyed the choir at the one service. As a result, many of the status quo discontinued their attendance and their support. But they did not leave the church. Rather, they waited in the background until either the pastor left or made a misstep.

Several months, two pastoral missteps and much tension later, the choir was reconstituted. This time, more participants swelled its ranks, almost in protest of the pastor's decision. "It would have been easier if I had had some indication of how much the spirit of that choir was still alive in this church," the pastor confided. He had in the inaugural enthusiasm of his tenure overlooked the choir ministry as a unique gift of this church. He would never do so again. An SCB could have been helpful by alerting the new pastor to an historical, anointed musical ministry that distinguished this church.

Step 2: Create a Sample SCB

Congregants often need an initial sample of an SCB to unleash their creative juices. Samples provide a structure, a configuration, and a demarcation of what you are proposing. However, this example should be just that—a model or pattern, but not a final SCB.

The temptation will be that when a leader presents a sample SCB, the hearers will marvel at how exacting and appropriate it is, suggesting it be accepted immediately. Regardless of their accolades, resist this temptation. Christians are usually a gracious people, and when this is coupled with being overworked, they may regard this example as sufficient and possibly even a godsend.

However, if leaders do not mull over the implications of the elements of an SCB, they will be more likely to overstep its boundaries. If they have not taken the time to closely consider and create each boundary, they will not be familiar enough with the boundaries to keep from crossing them. For the sake of effectiveness, all key leaders—clergy, lay, and informal—must be involved in crafting the SCB.

Unless a broad range of leaders is involved, there will not be sufficient goal ownership. Recently, the administrative pastor of a large church told about designing a newcomer program. He had read books, put together an elaborate PowerPoint training program, and filled this new ministry with people he knew in the church. "It lasted just a few months," said Barry. "The problem was, I did all the work for them. It was my idea, and there wasn't any room or need for their contributions. They didn't get to add their ideas. They had no goal ownership, and it died." A day later I was meeting with focus groups at this church. One group was comprised of new attendees. As we took turns speaking, the newcomers shared how difficult it had been to fit into the life of this church. I mentioned the previous newcomer ministry headed by Barry, to which one lady responded, "That was designed by someone who hasn't been a newcomer for a long time. It didn't give you things you needed, like a map of the church." "It wasn't focused on helping get people involved in things like Sunday school," responded another. "It was trying to get us back to church, not connecting us to a small group of people. People want a group where you can share your heart, not just fill a pew."

The conversations continued with other participants adding their input. Soon there was genuine enthusiasm about creating a more organic, newcomer-led guest ministry. Goal ownership was rising, and newcomers were seeing a way they could contribute at their new church. The key was participation and permission, not prescription and pronouncement.

For this reason, I shall not tender SCB samples. This might tempt the busy leader too greatly. Rather, this is such an important task, and the process outlined in such detail, that the leader should be able to craft his or her indigenous example. But ensure that your sample is just a model to foster creative juices.

In preparation for step 3, distribute to leaders the SCB sample, and ask them to come up with their own version (approximately the same length). Have them bring it to an upcoming meeting. Since their SCB should be nearly the same length as the sample, this can help you ascertain which areas are superfluous and which are crucial. If some elements of the sample are edited out by most participants, these elements are probably not widely accepted boundaries.

Step 3: Come Together to Compare Preliminary Statements

Participation. Participants should be selected from across the spectrum of lay and clergy people in the church. And as we'll see in chapter 8, it is important to get participation from both formal and informal leaders. These later participants are church members who have informal, behind-the-scenes power or influence. They often have long histories with the church and may be comprised of influential extended families.

However, if too many leaders are involved, the size of the meeting will be unwieldy. Thus, the goal should be representative participation. This means that representatives should be solicited from different voices and opinions in the church. They should be selected on three criteria:

1. Participants in the meeting that will craft an SCB should be congregants who have a gracious, conciliatory spirit—individuals who can find common ground and compromise. However, these characteristics are not enough, for they must also demonstrate traits 2 and 3 below.
2. The individuals who participate should be valid voices for a segment of the congregation. They should understand acutely the perspectives and worries of their group. But they should be able to graciously share perspectives with both sides and desire to find common ground.
3. They should be selected based on their ability to influence others within their segment of the church. Thus, they should be respected individuals whose opinions and conclusions others will consider.

Here then is an abbreviated list of potential representative participants:

- paid staff
- committee leaders
- volunteers in important positions, such as human resources, small group oversight and development, Christian education, Sunday school director, youth ministry, music ministry, etc.
- leaders of programs associated closely or housed within the church, such as a child development center, counseling clinic, school, daycare, preschool, high school, etc.
- leaders of long-standing or large Sunday school classes
- past leaders who helped the church through changes, such as building campaigns, outreach programs, mergers, staff selection

Size. It is also important that the number of participants does not make the meeting unwieldy. This is why participants should be representative, bringing to your meeting a representation of a segment of the congregation (even if their perspective is potentially antagonistic to your plans). The key to success is to balance size with representation.

A rule of thumb is to have twelve to sixteen participants, because a group of this size fosters interaction. This number however can be adjusted for overall size of the congregation, with larger congregations (four hundred plus in attendance) convening approximately twenty-six people. However, the small-group dynamics that foster interaction and transparency will break down if the group grows too large. Thus, a factor as noted above is to cultivate representative participation, while staying, if feasible, between twelve and sixteen participants.

Preparation. In step 2 we saw the homework was for all participants to use the sample SCB to draw up their own versions and bring them to the meeting. The responsibility to complete preliminary homework, and to bring it to the meeting, will need to be advertised and communicated before this meeting convenes.

Participants should be told they are being given only a sample SCB and that they should edit and adapt it as they see fit. They will then bring their statement to the meeting. This meeting will only be as successful as the completed and individual preliminary SCBs.

Step 4: Compile Preliminary Statements into a Rough Draft

Length. The meeting may take upwards of two hours, and thus two and a half hours should be designated. This process should not be hurried, for your SCB will have a long, influential effect on your future decisions.

Format. Ask each leader to read his or her preliminary statement without discussion or comment, even by the reader. This tactic gives everyone time to consider their colleagues' assessments and does not protract this initial exercise. It will be important for this rule to be maintained. Often churches have large cadres of people with the gift of teaching (Rom. 12:7). Thus, an inclination will be for these individuals to explain in detail the rationale for each of their boundaries. In addition, hearers will be tempted to attach their own commentaries. This results in a few participants sharing their initial SCBs. Explain the rationale for this no-comment rule and stick to it throughout the presentation of the homework.

After everyone has shared his or her initial SCB, list together on a board the recurring boundaries in the order of their frequency. This will give you an idea of perceived priorities and prevalence.

Goal. Craft the most prevalent boundaries along with additional insights into a draft SCB. Have this draft SCB typed and distributed to all participants within two business days.

Step 5: Conduct a Stakeholder Survey. Each Leader Will Present the Draft to Six Church Stakeholders

Homework. Once participants have received the draft SCB, have each approach six stakeholders and ask their input. The interviewer should write down each person's input and repeat it to ensure understanding. The leader should bring this input back to the next meeting.

Stakeholder Definition. Stakeholder is a term used in the management world that has helpful meaning for the church. Stakeholders are those who have an investment[7] (fiscal, emotional, or physical) in an organization. They have an interest in the success of an organization and are concerned about its future. The word *stakeholder* differs from the term *stockholder*, for stockholders have only financial claims upon the organization, whereas a stakeholder has a broader interest. Stakeholders can be volunteers, people who consider a church their church home, employees, long-standing members, a bank that loans the church money, and companies that provide the church with supplies.

Figure 7.1 gives a visual representation of the extensive nature of stakeholders.

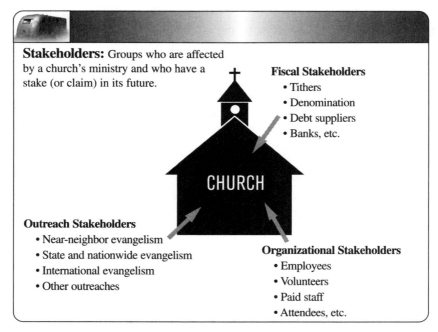

Stakeholders: Groups who are affected by a church's ministry and who have a stake (or claim) in its future.

Fiscal Stakeholders
- Tithers
- Denomination
- Debt suppliers
- Banks, etc.

CHURCH

Outreach Stakeholders
- Near-neighbor evangelism
- State and nationwide evangelism
- International evangelism
- Other outreaches

Organizational Stakeholders
- Employees
- Volunteers
- Paid staff
- Attendees, etc.

Survey Non-attendees. It is important that a stakeholder survey chart the feelings of people who have an interest in the congregation, but do not attend the church (for example fiscal and outreach stakeholders).

Examples can include neighbors near the church property, local business-people, community leaders, or denominational leaders.

Size of Survey. As can be seen from figure 7.1, there is a sizable web of individuals interested in the future of a church. This is why each of the twelve to twenty-six people involved in the creation of the SCB are asked to contact six individual stakeholders. The result is that the church can gain input from as many as 156 stakeholders.

Goal: Explain to meeting participants the expansive nature of the stakeholder population. In addition, use the graph and adds names to it to help them visualize the pervasive nature of the stakeholder realm.

Step 6: Analyze and Codify the Results of Your Stakeholder Survey

Length: This meeting should be the length of the meeting in step 5 (though a longer meeting may be necessary).

Format: This meeting should also parallel the above meeting in format. Initially allow everyone to share insights without comment, even by the presenter. After the presentations of the stakeholder survey have been made, list the boundaries that occur with the greatest frequency.

Goal: Again compile a list of change boundaries. Codify this into an SCB.

Permission: Different churches have different structures for approving declarations such as an SCB. (In chapter 8 we'll also see that the inclination for leaders to rush the boundary creation process can doom it.) Approach the proper democratic board in your congregation for final approval. If significant changes are incurred, reconvene the leaders for another session of compilation until a mutually agreeable SCB is created.

Step 7: Evaluate Your SCB at Three-month, Six-month and One-year Intervals

Evaluation is a critical part of the planning process and one churches too often ignore.[8] In addition, evaluation is needed more frequently at the initiation of a new strategy. Thus, convene meetings similar to the above but adjusted as necessary, on a regular basis with greater initial frequency. Subsequently, host this group at three-month, six-month, and one-year intervals and once yearly thereafter. However, schedule another meeting if there is a need to reconsider your evaluation or for additional insight.

Step 8: Display Your SCB

An SCB does little good if its contents are not widely known. Remember, the advantages of an SCB are twofold:

1. An SCB alleviates concern that change will go too far, because the limits (boundaries) of change have been described and decided upon (at least until further discussion changes them). Thus, the contents must be widely broadcast.

2. An SCB allows planners to ensure that they do not contemplate change that crosses predetermined boundaries of change for this congregation (until further discussion is held). Thus, planners must be familiar with change boundaries if they are to avoid them.

Part of this strategy will be to display your SCB in a location visible for church attendees and planners. Also, offer copies at this location so people can read it before launching new ideas and changes. Remember, it is the unexpected breadth of change that worries most people. When congregants and leaders have predefined boundaries that change will not traverse, congregations are more at ease with the process.

Include your SCBs with your church job descriptions and with volunteer recruitment and training. Make sure your leaders are clear about boundaries before they undertake congregational duties, and they will be less likely to cross them. Another idea is for denominational leaders to require SCBs within six months of the inauguration of a new pastorate.

ENERGIZED? GO SLOWLY

Clients of my consulting practice often find this SCB exercise energizing and stimulating. "Finally we are going to have limits to what should be changed," is how one older gentlemen described it. He was a leader in the congregation whose choir was terminated by an overzealous pastor.

Yet, the downfall of that zealous pastor's actions was not his intention (to reach out to baby boomers) or his method (using a modern worship expression), but rather his tempo. The pastor had moved too quickly, and in the process he had missed the informal boundaries within the congregation. Thus, in addition to establishing boundaries, leaders need to pace themselves, ensuring that change is neither conducted too quickly nor before consensus is established.

It is this measured, deliberate progress forward that we will discuss in chapter 8: "Go Slowly, Build Consensus, and Succeed."

QUESTIONS FOR GROUP STUDY

1. What are some unique giftings of your church? These are attributes recognized within your church, as well as in the community, as church strengths.
   - List them.
   - Prioritize them.
   - Create a draft list for all participants of the meeting to create an SCB.
2. Who do you think should participate in the group that creates your SCB?
   - Who are informal leaders?
   - Are informal leaders important?
   - Who are formal leaders?
   - Create a list of segments within your church. Find one person

from each segment who demonstrates maturity, graciousness, and respect. Use these names to create a list of twelve to twenty-six participants.

3. Who are the stakeholders in your organization? Create a representative sample from the categories below to define the expanse of your stakeholder sphere.

   - Who are the fiscal stakeholders?
   - Who are the organizational stakeholders?
   - Who are the outreach stakeholders?

4. How and where should your SCB be displayed to ensure it is effective in helping congregants understand boundaries for congregational change?

change reaction 1
you're trying to change things too fast!

the problem
church leaders have undertaken change in an unsteady or dis-unifying manner.

go slowly, build consensus, and succeed

"I didn't go into ministry to divide you, but to bring people together." Jim was visibly shaken by the turn of events at this church board meeting. As his wife watched, Jim, the pastor for only twenty months, was about to resign. I had been invited because a lay leader had read one of my books and hoped I could help.[1] However, the polarization had reached stage 5, and without a cooling of tempers, this church was headed toward not only Jim's leaving, but also a sizable exodus from the congregation.

"It's time for us to step back and take a look at this," suggested Stan, the layperson who had invited me. But before board members could respond, Jim continued. "It's clear I've let you down. I'm not going to cause any more friction. Sheri and I have decided to leave, and I'm putting in my resignation to the board right now." Jim nodded to his wife, Sheri, and she joined him. "We never meant to get you all divided. We just wanted to help. We've failed, but we appreciate your prayers for our future ministry."

Stunned silence greeted Jim's pronouncement, even though many board members had worried this was going to happen. Jim and Sheri left the room, and the board decided to reconvene Thursday night to decide on a course of action.

Thursday's meeting put more strain on this aging church. Only six months ago the church had begun to see an influx of younger generations, due largely to Jim and Sheri's hard work. The news of Jim's resignation had reverberated through the church community, and Thursday's meeting was three times as large as the Monday gathering. Everyone seemed discouraged over Jim's departure.

Over the course of the evening, two camps emerged. The first were traditionalists, whom I call the status quo. They are congregants who like the ministries and worship options a church has historically offered. Though they want the church to reach younger generations, they want to preserve the traditional worship expression and ministries. Plus, they were alarmed when Jim moved the 10:30 traditional service up to 9:45 to accommodate launching of a modern service. Sunday school had been at 9:30, and now many aging members found it difficult to get up and out to Sunday school at the new starting time: 8:45. Many board members felt Jim had forced through the new service times. Many congregants (and even some members of the board) felt Jim had circumvented them and their concerns. When attendance at the 9:45 service dropped 21 percent in three months, the status quo was alarmed. They didn't have a problem with the new service as much as they had a problem with the decrease in attendance and inconveniences it fostered (see figure 8.1). They felt Jim should have worked out a more amicable compromise, and they blamed him for not finding middle ground.

Previous Worship Service Times		New Worship Service Times
	8:45 9:00 9:15 9:30	Sunday School
Sunday School	9:45 10:00 10:15	Traditional Worshp Service
	10:30 10:45 11:00	
Blended Worship Service	11:15 11:30 11:45	Modern Worship Service
	12:00 12:15 12:30	

Similarly, those pushing for change didn't understand why the status quo was being so tough on Jim. The change proponents saw the new modern service at 11:15 as the salvation of this aging church. If anything, the change proponents would have liked their service a bit earlier, perhaps 10:45. The times had been worked out by Jim, who acted as a go-between among the status quo and the change proponents. Thus change proponents blamed Jim for not finding a harmonious solution. But they felt closer to Jim and Sheri than to the status quo, for Jim was more their age and embraced their preferences for modern music. To the change proponents, Jim was trying to rescue a church from itself. Though in their eyes Jim had mismanaged the process, they felt he was the best option for salvaging the church's future. To them Jim's resignation was a precursor to thoughts of leaving that they now entertained.

Little wonder Jim resigned. He felt animosity and disappointment from both factions. This was not why he had gone into the ministry. He had made mistakes, but now the factions appeared too pronounced and Jim was too weary.

"We've got to agree on both of these worship services," interjected Stan, who, though a member of the status quo, could see the importance of building consensus with the change proponents. "I've got a solution," began Carl, a new member who also played guitar for the modern worship service. "If people are truly interested in contemporary worship, then it has to be at 10:45 or 10:30. You won't reach people who like that style of worship at 11:15, when church isn't over till 12:30."

The roar of dissension drowned out the meeting for a moment, as I hurriedly scribbled my notes, hoping not to appear too callous as I chronicled the widening rift. Many jabs, defiant remarks, and sassy comments filled the room, until one board member tendered a comment that created the breaking point.

"If that's what you want to do," announced George, a member of the status quo, "you ought to go somewhere else and do it." For a moment the clamor subsided. But it soon recurred, though now with less intensity. The gauntlet had been cast, and the change proponents had to decide if they would accept the challenge and strike out on their own.

Though the meeting concluded forty-five minutes later with terse but cordial goodbyes, the many parking lot gatherings indicated that little resolution had resulted.

This is from an actual church scenario, but pseudonyms were used to protect anonymity. However, the story in various permutations has occurred all across America.

Soon the change proponents joined a nearby growing church, and within eight months the modern service was discontinued. "We didn't expect people to get so upset," recalled Stan. "But Jim made things worse." I explained to Stan that I believed the fault did not primarily lie with Pastor Jim. Jim had never been schooled in the mechanics and processes of change, and as a result he and his family had fallen prey to the insidious polarization that mismanaged change can produce.

SIX STAGES AND FIVE TRIGGERS OF CHANGE

Many management scholars also happen to be committed laypersons in their churches. As a result, some have investigated how research into organizational change can throw light upon these processes in the church. Two such management scholars are Bruno Dyck and Frederick Starke at the University of Manitoba. One of the most researched processes is why change proponents leave an organization.[2]

In the business world losing your change proponents can be costly. For example, Jeff Hawkins, inventor of the Personal Digital Assistant (PDA), left Palm Computing in 1998 two years after the successful debut of his Palm Pilot PDA. Hawkins, by some reports, was frustrated by corporate meddling from 3Com, which had purchased Palm Computing in 1997. Hawkins and strategic planner Donna Dubinsky founded Handspring in 1998, where they were free to implement their new ideas. As a result, Hawkins created the highly success-ful Handspring Visor PDA in 1999. Palm Computing began losing market share so quickly to the upstart Handspring Company and its founder Hawkins, that Palm had to buy back Handspring to become profitable again (and to regain Hawkins, the change proponent, they had lost). The result of losing Hawkins, Dubinsky, and their creative ideas proved costly for 3Com.[3]

Well versed in these status-quo or change-proponent tensions, Dyck and Starke undertook a study of churches in Canada. In doing so, they uncovered a six-stage polarization process. They found the critical factors are the triggers that push a church out of one stage into the next stage. When they analyzed the process, they found that in churches that retained their change proponents only two triggers of the five triggers were expe-rienced differently. Thus if churches could just identify where they were in the change process and change just two triggers, churches could keep their change proponents and their status quo in relative harmony.[4]

When a colleague introduced me to the research of Dyck and Starke, it was revelatory. These were the research-based insights that had eluded me, and which so many of my clients encountered. I thus wrote a book explaining this process for church leaders and giving examples from my client congregations (albeit anonymously again). I also showed how church leaders can discover which stage they are in and how they can substitute a positive trigger for the usual negative one. Titled *Staying Power: Why People Leave the Church Over Change and What You Can Do about It*, according to my students, this is my most important book.

However, for the present discussion I am going to give a brief overview of the six-stage, five-trigger process to help church leaders grasp some of the lessons from that book.

How Churches Change: Stages, Triggers, and Two Routes

Stages and Triggers. Stages are phases or episodes a church goes through. In each stage, churches behave in a similar way. And in each stage, the process is progressive, meaning it is always moving forward unless something occurs to stop the forward progress and get the church on a different route.

A *trigger* is a force, usually an event, that pushes the church forward into the next stage. The key to managing the change process is to understand the next trigger and avoid it (or substitute a harmonizing trigger) to prevent the church from moving forward on an erroneous route.

Route A (Toward Group Exit) and Route B (Toward Group Retention). There are two routes a church can take through the change process.

Route A leads to polarization and usually departure of change proponents.

Route B occurs when the change process is managed better and relative harmony results. On Route B, change proponents stay in the church and the church grows as it reaches more generations with more cultural options.

Route A: Where Change Leads to Division and Departure

Let us first look at the six stages and five triggers on Route A, where division and departure result.

Stage 1: Relative Harmony. In this stage the church is fairly united and there is little dissension. Though there is growing awareness some change must be undertaken, there are few concrete ideas on how to do this. While the congregation is living harmoniously, the harmony is relative, for fallible humans never truly live harmoniously.

Trigger 1: Conflicting Ideas Event. The change process begins when a new idea is introduced, often by congregants who attend some event that proposes ideas that conflict with the way the church is doing things.

In the example that began this chapter, Carl and a few other church members had attended a seminar on how to start a modern worship service. The process was so well laid out that Carl and the other attendees returned to the church excited about implementing their ideas.

Stage 2: Idea Development. Once Carl and the others returned, they began to share their ideas with other likeminded congregants. Their enthusiasm grew, for they saw this as a way to attract more people of their generation and help an aging church survive. They believed all members would rejoice at this prospect.

Trigger 2: Negative Legitimizing Event. Here the process goes awry. The change proponents had codified their ideas, drafted up a proposal, and delegated responsibilities so the modern worship could be implemented. They knew everyone at the church was overworked, so they sought to have their plans and volunteers in place before they approached Pastor Jim. The excitement and anticipation among the change proponents began to rise as they saw their ideas as essential for the church's survival. "Surely everyone would be excited about this," recalled a change proponent.

The change proponents first approached Pastor Jim because he was nearly their age and was seen as sympathetic. But here a fatal mistake occurred. Pastor Jim was excited about the prospect of a new worship celebration that was already staffed and organized. This was what the church needed, and Jim did not have to worry about anything. I'm told Carl asked Jim, "What do you think?" To which Jim responded, "Sounds great! We've got to run this by the church board, but I don't think there will be any problems." Carl and the other change proponents left the meeting ecstatic. The fruition of their planning and research had paid off. In their minds the church would soon have what the change proponents needed for worship and what the church needed to survive.

On the surface this would seem like a positive legitimizing event, for Pastor Jim had legitimized their process with encouraging remarks. But in actuality, a perceived unbridled enthusiasm by Jim for this new idea actually sank the idea—and Jim's pastorate. The way Jim legitimized this event started the change proponents moving forward too fast and too far.

The status quo felt overlooked and ignored as they heard about changes that would affect the entire church. If Pastor Jim had slowed the change proponents, helped them seek permission, and brought reticent status quo congregants on board, change could have occurred in a positive fashion. But first let us continue to consider this process on Route A toward division.[5]

Stage 3: Change. Change proponents set about creating the change they feel they have been given permission to pursue. Pent-up energies and longings for such a change foster passion and speed. Permission is seen as a formality, and the status quo are not seriously consulted.

In Pastor Jim's church the status quo was beginning to feel left out and avoided. When Carl came to the church board to seek permission, his plans had been made. Carl's presentation of his proposal, strongly supported by Pastor Jim, seemed like a formality to status quo board members, rather than a sincere desire for input and permission. The status quo was initially and reluctantly tolerant.

Trigger 3: Alarm Event. At some point, change always infringes upon the status quo. When this happens, it often alarms the defenders of the status quo. Often this occurs when the change proponents push too hard or too fast. The result is that the status quo was alarmed and began to meet separately as a group.

The change proponents initiated an alarm event when Carl returned to the church board a second time to argue that worship times must be changed to accommodate the modern service. Moving the traditional service up from 10:30 to 9:45 (figure 8.1) did not seem to Carl and other change proponents a significant sacrifice for the status quo. But because Carl and many change proponents did not attend Sunday school, they did not sense the inconvenience of starting Sunday school at 8:45 as keenly as did the status quo.

When the status quo and their Sunday school class heard about the change, and how Carl with the support of Pastor Jim had pushed this decision through the church board, the status quo began to have its own meetings to discuss what could be done.

Stage 4: Resistance. Two factions now form, as a change proponent subgroup is joined by a status quo subgroup intent on preventing the change. "We had to do something," recalled George. "The change proponents were not interested in us."

The status quo now undergo group identification. In the example above they were known as the Highlighters, named after the Highlighter Sunday school, a large Sunday school class of senior adults. This name now became attached to all congregants who were dissatisfied with the time changes.

The change proponents for the first time see opposition to plans they had expected to be conflict free. Meetings and discussions behind their backs alarms change proponents, and they begin to muster support for their views. The result is that two sides have now coalesced in the church, and neither is talking directly to the other.

The go-between became Pastor Jim. He tried to placate both sides, but since his information was always second hand, assumptions, presumptions, and suspicions continued to push the status quo and change proponents further apart.

Trigger 4: Polarization Event. As Julius Caesar said as he invaded the Roman homeland, "the die is cast," meaning that the chain of events is now almost inescapable.

A polarization event occurs when, usually at a meeting, emotional intensity peaks. The factions are now visibly apparent and at odds. In the midst of the arguing over where and how the process has gone wrong, the pastor is often caught in the middle. To the pastor each side seems to be blaming him or her for the polarization. Each of the pastor's actions, comments, encouragements, and mistakes is duly noted, with each side frustrated by a rehashing of their journey to schism.

Dyck and Starke found that at this stage the pastor often resigns, as did Pastor Jim. This is because pastors enter the ministry not for such times or for such blame. Pastors seek to be peacemakers and intermediaries. Thus when the polarization process occurs, the pastor may feel he or she must be the go-between. If the process goes amiss, the pastor will feel like he or she has failed in a central aspect of the pastoral duty.

As I mentioned earlier, pastors need not feel thus. This is not their fault as much as it is a lack of knowledge regarding the change process (more on this in chapter 9). Still, Pastor Jim felt at fault, and his resignation was the culmination of his attempt to manage change.

Instead of decreasing polarization, however, Jim's resignation increased it.

Stage 5: Intense Conflict. Just when you think conflict could not escalate more, frustrations over trigger 4, the polarization event, push the split forward. Intense emotions throughout the church create a stage for escalating clashes. Not always does a pastor resign at trigger 4, but regardless, the trigger unleashes criticism and finger pointing on both sides. Starke and Dyck found this stage often accompanied by nasty letters and meetings characterized by name-calling and shouting.[6]

Congregants would never have envisioned that in such a short span of time they would be in such discord. In hindsight the pastor receives an even worse reputation, as the intense conflict is seen largely as a legacy of the pastor's tenure.

Trigger 5: Justifying Event. The status quo usually gives change proponents a final ultimatum. In our scenario, this occurred when George blurted out, "It that's what you want to do, then you ought to go somewhere else and do it." This was the provocation that gave Carl and other change proponents justification to leave.

The change proponents saw that the die was cast. Soon Carl and the other change proponents would feel they had permission to break away from the church.

Stage 6: Group Exit. Change proponents often leave the parent organization and form a breakaway organization. Dyck and Starke describe this as "a breakaway organization forms when a group of organization members, frustrated by their inability to implement change in their parent organization, leave it and start up a new organization in which they are free to implement their ideas."[7] Initially euphoric, change proponents often lose their identity if they are absorbed into another church, or they may fail to survive if they strike out on their own as a new congregation.

The status quo, however, feels abandoned. While the change proponents left to join a nearby, innovative congregation, the status quo labored along, trying to attract younger generations but with a growing reputation that they were not welcoming to those they wanted to reach. The result was that the church nearly died, though eventually it welcomed in younger generations and thrived as a multigenerational church.

Route B: Change Brings About Unity

Route B, resulting in the retention of change proponents, occurs because just two triggers are handled differently. Let's look at how triggers 2 and 4, when handled differently, result in unity rather than dispersion.

Stage 1: Relative Harmony. This stage is the same on Route B toward group retention. The congregation is relatively unified and united in purpose.

Trigger 1: Conflicting Ideas Event. Here again the trigger is identical on Route B. Congregants who will become change proponents, attend a seminar, read a book, or in another manner become exposed to an idea that conflicts with the way things are done. As in Route A, the conflicting event stimulates ideas that the change proponents feel would benefit the congregation.

Stage 2: Change. This stage is identical on both routes as well, with new ideas and strategies percolating within the change proponents. The change proponents begin to coalesce into a group to bring about these changes.

Trigger 2: Positive Legitimizing Event. Here is one of the two triggers that is handled differently in organizations that stay united. Below are the five keys to fostering a *positive* legitimizing event:

- **Key 1—Don't get excited.** On Route B toward group retention, the pastor is careful not to give the passionate change proponents too much encouragement too soon, for the pastor knows they will run with this new idea too far and too fast.
- **Key 2—Seek permission.** The pastor cautiously advises change proponents that administrative committees and channels must be consulted, seeking permission and input.
- **Key 3—Move ahead slowly.** Now the process moves ahead slowly, allowing the status quo to understand the rationale behind strategies for change.
- **Key 4—Get outside help.** Dyck and Starke found that often an outside facilitator, such as a denominational leader or consultant, was used to slow the process and help change proponents get input and gain permission.[8]
- **Key 5—Listen to reticent members.** Another key is to listen to reticent members and hear their concerns. Usually pastors know who these reticent and standoffish people are, yet because consulting them is not pleasurable, we usually avoid them. Avoiding them dooms the process. They must be consulted and allowed to share their concerns. In fact, I have found that listening to reticent members not only diffuses their distance and frustration, but also opens direct communication channels between the status quo and the change proponents. Change proponents get involved in the permission process, listening to the concerns of apprehensive and reticent congregants. Communication between those pushing for change and the status quo is improved. The pastor is not caught in the middle,

because he or she encourages change proponents to go directly to reticent status quo people whom the pastor has helped identify.

In the scenario that began this chapter, Pastor Jim could have asked change proponents to meet with several leaders privately and listen to their concerns. This might have included several members of the Highlighters class. Jim should have encouraged change proponents to understand that their good ideas would be doomed if pushed too fast or too far. Books and articles that explain the process should be used to acquaint change proponents with the change process. Change proponents do not want people (including themselves) to leave the church, and they usually will be willing to go slower and build consensus when they realize this is necessary to foster unity and bring about change.

Then, before the change proponents met with the board, they could have drawn a plan that addressed the concerns of the status quo. If problems arose, Pastor Jim could have brought in a denominational leader or a church consultant to assist.

Stage 3: Change. Change now occurs in much the same way as before. The change proponents form a group to bring about the change, and the status quo are generally tolerant.

Trigger 3: Alarm Event. This happens on both routes, though all church leaders wish it would not. But the alarm event is inevitable. At some point change will bring tension and discomfort. When wed with inconvenience, change always alarms some. Thus the alarm event is inescapable. Don't expect to have effortless or conflict-free change; it rarely happens.

Stage 4: Resistance. Just as an alarm event is unavoidable, so is the resistance that will rise from it. Again, this cannot be avoided. But it can be managed by how you handle the next critical trigger.

Trigger 4: Harmonizing Event. This is the other key trigger (along with trigger 2) that is handled differently on Route B. Unlike trigger 4 in Route A, trigger 4 here can become a harmonizing event, focusing on finding compromise and common ground. There are two general characteristics to this event:

Compromise. The harmonizing event creates a high degree of compromise behavior. Thus change proponents should be aware from the beginning that when resistance surfaces, they must be prepared to compromise for the good of the organization.

Unity in diversity. The second key element is that the harmonizing event emphasizes the overall organizational identity. The bigger picture is highlighted, and the diversity of the congregation via various generations, ethnicities, or other subcultures is celebrated. Here we return to Peter Wagner's image of a stew pot rather than Andrew Greeley's image of the American melting pot. Wagner reminds us that North America is not really a melting pot, any more than our churches are. For rather than resulting in some unappetizing gray-green goo, a stew pot brings up the image of a tasty mixture, where each ingredient adds its unique flavor while retaining its own unique properties. The stew pot creates an image of "a new product, colorful and flavorful to a degree that would have been impossible for any of the ingredients taken alone."[9]

Such harmonizing events are usually facilitated by the pastor, church leaders, an outside consultant, or a denominational leader. Their goal is to remind people that they can accomplish more together than apart and that arriving at unity through compromise is an important element of church life.[10]

Stage 5: Dissonant Harmony. As a musician I first chaffed at the idea of a stage called *dissonant harmony*, for it reminds me of my mistake-laden early piano efforts. Then I am reminded of the beautiful and powerful atonal music of Anton Webern, Arnold Schoenberg, and others. Their music created tension-filled, yet rewarding musical landscapes. While never comfortable, their music has a beauty about it.

The same is true of the church. While change brings about tension and strain, it stretches us for the better. In fact, dissonant harmony may be the preferred outcome of the change process. The situation is not totally harmonious, for the harmony is accompanied by some disagreement and apprehension. But, this is inevitable when fallible humans are involved.

Conflict and tension were in part responsible for the spread of the good news of the gospel. Jesus' disciples in Jerusalem were content to stay in the Jewish capital, even though Jesus had commanded that they should "make disciples of all nations" (Matt. 28:19). Not until they experienced heightened persecution by the Romans did the disciples disperse and spread the good news throughout the Roman Empire (Acts 8:1; 11:19). Change was not pleasant or easy. But it was necessary. Thankfully, God directs His people in less vigorous ways as well.

Trigger 5: Does Not Occur. Now, rather than a trigger pushing the congregation into the next phase, there is a slow and unhurried evolution into Stage 6: Group Retention.

Stage 6: Group Retention. The result of a journey on Route B is greater understanding within the church, better communication, and group retention.

GO SLOWLY, BUILD CONSENSUS, AND SUCCEED

From the research of management scholars Dyck, Starke, and others, we can see that a measured, prudent, conciliatory, harmonizing process of introducing change is necessary for change to succeed. Here, then, are several principles for ushering in change to a congregation.

Do not get too excited too soon. Remember, you do not want to overly and thus negatively legitimize new ideas. Rather, cautiously appreciate the efforts of change proponents, and outline for them the administrative permission processes and the next steps to undertake.

Go to reticent members, listening to their concerns. This does four things:

1. It creates a direct communication link between change proponents and the status quo.
2. Reticent status quo members feel like they have a voice when they are approached with authenticity and genuineness.

3. Everyone has time to consider the nuances of a change.

4. Compromise and creativity can be fostered by listening to varied voices.[11]

Get permission. Once you have a change strategy that has been considered and commented upon by various segments of the church, take it to the decision-making body.

Go slowly. Do not rush the process. The larger a church is, the more complex its communication channels.

Don't be long on talk and short on action. Again it is important to not only build consensus but to move forward at a measured, steady pace. Each church will have a different cadence. To discover your individual tempo, look at how change was handled in the past, both successfully and unsuccessfully. You can ascertain from your history the tempo for effective change that best suits your congregation.

Focus on unity in diversity. Celebrate the varied contributions of the body of Christ. 1 Corinthians 12:4–7, 12, 14–20 reads:

> There are different kinds of gifts, but the same Spirit. There are different kinds of service, but the same Lord. There are different kinds of working, but the same God works all of them in all men. Now to each one the manifestation of the Spirit is given for the common good . . . . The body is a unit, though it is made up of many parts; and though all its parts are many, they form one body. So it is with Christ . . . . Now the body is not made up of one part but of many. If the foot should say, "Because I am not a hand, I do not belong to the body," it would not for that reason cease to be part of the body. And if the ear should say, "Because I am not an eye, I do not belong to the body," it would not for that reason cease to be part of the body. If the whole body were an eye, where would the sense of hearing be? If the whole body were an ear, where would the sense of smell be? But in fact God has arranged

the parts in the body, every one of them, just as he wanted them to be. If they were all one part, where would the body be? As it is, there are many parts, but one body.

Be ready to go through the process again. The process is cyclical. With each new idea the six-stage, five-trigger process begins again. This is why it is important for church and denominational leaders to become familiar with this model for change. It is not usually comfortable, but it is necessary.

QUESTIONS FOR GROUP STUDY

Consider your church history, and note how change has been handled poorly in the past. Did you see the following stages and triggers? Write a few sentences about each stage and trigger. Then discuss the results.

		Your Observations:
Stage 1: Relative Harmony		
Trigger 1: Conflicting Ideas Event. A new idea is introduced that some people believe will help the church.	**R**	
Stage 2: Idea Development. A group begins to form around this new idea.	**O**	
Trigger 2: Negative Legitimizing Event. Someone inadvertently gives the change proponents too much encouragement, and they move forward too far or too fast.	**U** **T** **E**	
Stage 3: Change. Change begins to take place.	**A**	
Trigger 3: Alarm Event. Some event alarms the status quo, and they begin to meet to discuss this.		

		Your Observations:
Stage 4: Resistance. The status quo now mount efforts to slow down or stop the change.	**R**	
Trigger 4: Polarization Event. Emotional intensity peaks, and the pastor or other leaders are blamed for the disunity the church experiences.	**O**	
Stage 5: Intense Conflict. Criticism and finger pointing ensue, sometimes accompanied by nasty letters and meetings characterized by name calling and shouting.	**U** **T** **E**	
Trigger 5: Justifying Event. Change proponents are given an ultimatum.	**A**	
Stage 6: Group Exit. Change proponents leave the church and either form a separate organization or join a like-minded congregation.		

Consider your church history and note how change has been handled successfully in the past. Did you see the following stages and triggers? Write a few sentences about each stage and trigger. Then discuss the results.

		Your Observations:
Stage 1: Relative Harmony	**R**	
Trigger 1: Conflicting Ideas Event. A new idea is introduced that some people believe will help the church.	**O**	
Stage 2: Change. A group begins to form around this new idea.	**U** **T**	
Trigger 2: Positive Legitimizing Event. Permission is sought, input is solicited, compromise is fostered; and though progress is slow, it is steady.	**E** **B**	

		Your Observations:
Stage 3: Change. Change begins to take place.	**R**	
Trigger 3: Alarm Event. Some event alarms the status quo, and they begin to meet together to discuss situation.	**O**	
Stage 4: Resistance. The status quo now mount efforts to slow down or stop the change.	**U**	
Trigger 4: Harmonization Event. Compromise is sought, and unity in diversity is emphasized.	**T E**	
Stage 5: Dissonant Harmony. Though there is tension, there is no combative behavior, shouting, or name calling.	**B**	
Stage 6: Group Retention. The change proponents remain within the church, and the church is stronger as a result.		

part four

CHURCH CHANGE IN THE FUTURE

train
for
change

Phil was headed to seminary—again. "I'm not called to this," he said as he prepared to leave a congregation he had shepherded for seven years. "The work of organizing this church is beyond me, and I've got better things to do with my time and skills."

Phil was a personable, smart, and well-liked pastor, but his organizational skills were sub par. He sought to micromanage a new congregation in a fast-growing suburb of a metropolitan area. Though he had introduced many good ideas, at the conclusion of his ministry church leaders were frustrated with his management style. "We've got two options," said Steve, a lay leader. "Close or do it all over again. This has been the history here. We've grown and divided, grown and divided."

Phil's failure was not lack of intellect, perseverance, care, or will. In fact, Phil was intelligent and was now returning to seminary to work on a doctorate in theology. No one questioned that he had a superior intellect and a personable nature. Pastor Phil's deficiency was the kind of knowledge he possessed. Entering seminary the first time, he had taken the standard required courses in the master of divinity program. The courses emphasized theology, church history, preaching, counseling, and apologetics. The curriculum he took was weak on management. The result was that Phil was a good counselor and an engaging, theologically sound preacher. But deficient understanding of church management led to his eventual ousting.

Steve's appraisal reminded me that Phil was the second pastor newly out of seminary who had left this church in the past decade. Both new pastors had tried to capitalize on the church's location in a growing suburb. However, without basic management skills, both pastors' intentions, passions, and intellects were not enough. They were trained, but only partially.

I remarked to a colleague recently that more pastors are forced out of a church because of poor management skills than because of poor theology. My colleague, a theology professor, remarked with a twinkle in his eye, "Well, maybe they should be forced out due to bad theology."

MINISTERIAL EDUCATION FOR A NEW MILLENNIUM

The Problem May Be Training

As we saw earlier, postmodern Gen-Xers value experience over head knowledge. For example, you'll recall that upper-middle-class students Mike Yankoski and Sam Purvis left college to live as homeless people to understand the plight of homelessness in America.[1]

Yet, many colleges and seminaries are embedded in the waning modern era, a period that began with the Enlightenment and extends to today. Remember that in the modern era, head knowledge is preferred over physical experience. Conversely, for those influenced by the *post*modern era, experience is usually preferred over head knowledge.[2] So, seminaries may have historically erred on the side of providing theoretical knowledge rather than practical experience. While this is changing,[3] it is important to note that in many cases (but not all), seminary education may be weak in training pastors in both knowledge and experience of management skills.

Thus, the fault lies not in pastors when they are untrained in management skills, though, it is easy for congregants to blame them for their lack of managerial proficiency. Yet, I have not found pastors averse to management training. They are untutored or unaware of the insights the management sciences can offer. Thus, pastors, in my view, are not the primary impediment.

Rather, the problem may lie with educators such as myself, for in the past our programs have leaned toward equipping the pastor to be the philosophical shepherd of a spiritual organization. Instead, we must acknowledge what theologian Emil Brunner recognized: the church is both a *spiritual fellowship* or *supernatural organization* that requires shepherding and also an *organizational fellowship* or *administrative organization* that must be managed, administered, and united toward common and biblical goals.[4] As a result, many of us in graduate schools are diligently seeking to strengthen the management component in ministerial training programs.

Let us look briefly at a few attempts.

Changes in Ministerial Training

Many changes on the horizon are making seminary and graduate education more management sensitive. The Association of Theological Schools, the accrediting body for seminaries, has permitted new, hands-on courses and degrees to be developed. Schools such as Indiana Wesleyan University, Fuller Theological Seminary, Asbury Theological Seminary,

Regent University, and others have integrated management into the curriculum of ministerial training. In fact, at Indiana Wesleyan University, we have designed online and onsite master of arts degrees in ministry leadership that include management skills. We believe such holistic training is critical for developing spiritual and organizational "world-changers." There are plans to expand this synergetic relationship.

In the business world, practical degrees such as the master of arts in business administration (MBA) are in demand. Since the 1970s, business professors have known that developing business students' knowledge with case studies is as important as theoretical knowledge. Now the ministerial training world is beginning to see the validity of this approach. Plus, evaluation of pastors often shows they fail in early pastorates because of a trial-and-error learning process with church management skills.[5] To prevent the unwanted killing of churches by inexperienced pastors learning their trade, educators are increasing practical segments of ministerial preparation.

A PASTOR-BUSINESSPERSON PARTNERSHIP

The question now becomes, what can be done to help current pastors nurtured in theological education gain practical knowledge of how to manage churches. We have seen in this book that practical knowledge, in addition to theoretical knowledge, is needed to ensure healthy and unified change.

The answer may be a partnership between the lay businessperson (who serves as a volunteer leader in the church) and the pastor, in which both individuals share knowledge, broaden understanding, and contribute strengths.

The pastor can help the volunteer leader understand the implications of church history, theology, and doctrine. Many pastors have regular meetings with key leaders to emphasize New Testament history, theology, and denominational distinctives. Yet, these can be tedious and or disconnected if not tied to a reciprocal sharing of knowledge.

The volunteer church leader should reciprocate. This means the volunteer—if skilled in management—should reciprocate by sharing his or her management knowledge with the pastor.

Four Common Fallacies

Unfortunately, I have noticed lay businesspersons offer excuses that often inhibit them from sharing their knowledge. Let's look at each briefly.

Fallacy 1: Business Principles Don't Apply to the Church. The church is an organization that must be managed and a community that must be shepherded. You will recall that theologian Emil Brunner, as well as management scholars such as Roger Finke and Rodney Stark, pointed out when godly and appropriate management tools are applied to the church, the church grows and is healthy.[6] Also management scholars such as Dyck and Starke have demonstrated how process models of group exit behavior can help church leaders effectively manage change.[7] Thus some, but not all, business principles do apply to the church.

Fallacy 2: The Pastor Is the Church Expert. Again, the pastor may appear to be the expert due to his or her knowledge in theology, Bible, history, and denominationalism. But, pastors are not usually knowledgeable in the complementary area of management.

Fallacy 3: The Pastor Is Not Interested. Because pastors tend to be consumed with the many tasks of church leadership,[8] they may appear to be uninterested in acquiring new knowledge; new knowledge or experience can be viewed by a pastor as adding to his or her already overloaded duties. However, when a businessperson demonstrates that management tools can lighten the pastor's load and make the organization more efficient, pastors will usually embrace management insights.

Fallacy 4: I Haven't Been a Christian Very Long. In this scenario, a businessperson is concerned that he or she might unknowingly introduce something unbiblical to the church. But because pastors are steeped in theology, church history, and denominational viewpoints, they can sift through management ideas and tell which ones have potential to help and which might damage the church. I have found pastors to be open to new ideas (even, as we saw in chapter 8, too much so at times). Also, because of their intellectual bent, pastors are often open to new management synergies and alliances.

So give your pastor a chance. Don't write off your management insights until you have shared them. But remember to let the pastor come to his or her own conclusion regarding the viability of each suggestion. Most pastors, like Pastor Phil whose story began this chapter, go into the ministry because they have sharp and exacting minds. They usually can tell when an idea is appropriate or inappropriate.

Six Steps to Building a Pastor-Businessperson Partnership for Change

Step 1: Merge Your Knowledge. Approach your pastor humbly and offer to brainstorm management principles that might be helpful in the church context. Remember, neither the pastor nor the layperson will be knowledgeable in both secular management and church management. Thus, this process will require both pastor and church volunteer to learn together. Neither will have all the right answers, but together they can discover the right strategies and tactics.

Step 2: Study Each Other's Disciplines. The businessperson must become acquainted with boundaries from church history, theology, and orthodoxy. The church leader will want to acquaint volunteer leaders with the basics of denominational distinctives, orthodox theology, and pitfalls that have been surmounted in church history. And the volunteer leader will want to provide the pastor with helpful books, articles, and insights the business leader has encountered.

I have often found it helpful if businesspeople in the congregation link with the pastor in a reciprocal book study. In other words, the businessperson suggests a management book that has been helpful, and together they read a chapter each week. Then they come together regularly to discuss what they are reading.

Either concurrently or consecutively, the pastor can suggest a book on theology, church history, spiritual disciplines, or some other appropriate topic that the pastor and layperson read together and discuss. What results is a pastor-businessperson ideas exchange on the twin topics of church management and theological shepherding.

Step 3: Reciprocate Through Conferences and Seminars. This is one of the most productive steps I have encountered. Pastors are renowned for encouraging church volunteers to attend seminars and workshops on new ministry strategies and tactics. Because pastors are often strategic big-picture leaders, they want to expose their leaders to new ideas via workshops and clinics. Plus, this is needed if the volunteer church leader is to gain a knowledge of creative opportunities for the church.

The businessperson should reciprocate by inviting the pastor to attend management seminars where the pastor can learn firsthand from business professionals. Bringing your pastor to a seminar allows the pastor to ask questions about how these management ideas can be applied in the church context. As a result, pastors are often able to adapt ideas more readily to the church context.

Step 4: Work on Each Other's Plans. As the layperson's business plans begin to emerge, the pastor can add his or her burgeoning knowledge and advice. And, as the pastor begins to develop strategic plans for the church, the layperson can add his or her insights. Thus, submitting plans to one another creates a feedback loop in which leaders from the business realm and the church realm learn and critique together. The result is greater understanding, insight, and appreciation.

Step 5: Evaluate Together. Evaluation is critical for adjusting strategy and tactics, but is usually missing in our churches. To ensure that evaluation is not overlooked in your partnership between management and church leadership, host regular times to evaluate what you are doing.

Step 6: Repeat the Process. This six-step process is cyclical. Once you have completed steps 1–5, repeat them. Leaders who are evaluating together should be ready to go back to step 1 and merge their knowledge again. After merging knowledge, they must study more deeply one another's disciplines (step 2). Then move on to step 3 with a reciprocation of seminars and workshops, and so on. This will ensure that knowledge of church volunteers and pastors is constantly increasing. The process becomes a partnership for knowledge expansion and transfer from two related professions.

The result is that the church has laypeople more acquainted in the nuances and principles of church leadership, and the church has pastors increasingly acquainted with applicable management principles.

One Important Caveat

At this juncture let me say in the strongest terms that because business management is based on a fiscal model, not all management principles will apply to the church. There are still, however, a plethora of management principles in the areas of conflict management, volunteer recruitment, cultural adaptation, and change that are pertinent and important for the church. To distinguish between which management principles are irrelevant and which are pertinent, evaluation by both management leaders and pastoral leaders is needed.

QUESTIONS FOR GROUP STUDY

1. List church volunteers (i.e., laypeople) in the congregation who have success in the business world.
2. Contact the individuals on your list.
   - Ask them how familiar they are with management principles, management thinking, and management theories.
   - Ask if they have studied, taken courses, or attended seminars on business management.

- Rank their experience and insight, using the following guidelines.

    1 **very low** degree of management knowledge

    2 **low** degree of management knowledge

    3 **moderate** degree of management knowledge

    4 **somewhat high** degree of management knowledge

    5 **very high** degree of management knowledge

3. Evaluate what you think should be done with your list.

    - Are there businesspersons on this list with whom church leaders already have a relationship?
    - Have these individuals been active in the church in the past?
        - Is so, are they active today? If not why not?
        - If they are still active, what are they doing?
        - Could they be better used by creating a partnership between them and pastoral leadership?

4. Contact the five most promising individuals from your list. Solicit one or two to work with one or two church pastors in developing a businessperson-pastor partnership using the six steps to building a pastor-businessperson partnership.

change reaction 1
what are you doing to help
us change, Pastor?

the problem
conscientious congregational
leaders realize that negative
change reactions are possible
and seek ways to remain
unified during the process.

stay connected to those you serve

This book has a dual audience. It is intended to be used by church volunteers (i.e., laypersons) as well as by professional church leaders (i.e., clergy, pastors, ecclesial professionals). In most chapters this duality is reflected. However, this chapter is especially important for *both* groups to absorb and digest, because the ideas in this book are all doomed to fail—even destabilize your organization—if leaders do not make a conscientious effort to stay connected to those they serve. Congregants expect the pastor to take the lead in this endeavor.

ORGANIC LEADERSHIP

What do we call such critical and connected leadership? There is a great deal of talk today about the type of leadership that should be reflected in churches: coach, visionary, team-builder, or executive, to name a few. While all these designations are helpful, there is a term for leadership that resonates in both biblical and management circles: *organic*.

The term *organic* originally pertained to the organs of the human body. But over time this definition has been expanded to refer to anything interconnected, cohesive, and tied to its roots.[1]

Such imagery is employed in Scripture to refer to the interdependent, cohesive, and living aspects of a healthy and growing church. First Corinthians 12 (vv. 12, 14, 20, and 27) is Paul's vigorous reminder that a church must have varied yet complementary gifts to function. "The body is a unit, though it is made up of many parts; and though all its parts are many, they form one body. So it is with Christ" (v. 12). Romans 12:4–6a expands this thought, "Just as each of us has one body with many members, and these members do not all have the same function, so in Christ we who are many form one body, and each member belongs to all the others. We have different gifts, according to the grace given us." This is organic imagery.

But organic is not limited to churches; it is used in sociology and anthropology to denote inter-reliant, grounded organizations. Perhaps the most pervasive use is in the political sciences, where Antonio Gramsci labeled as an *organic intellectual* a person so connected to those he or she served that the person could explain grand concepts in simple and clear imagery. For Gramsci the organic intellectual was not limited to politics, but included playwrights, novelists, journalists, and religious leaders.[2]

QUALITIES OF ORGANIC LEADERSHIP

Organic provides a useful designation for a church and its leadership that are inter-reliant, connected, organized, and tied to those they serve. Let's look at each one of these attributes and at how organic leadership can help a church tackle change.

Organic Leaders Are Inter-Reliant

Inter-Reliance and Leadership. Church leaders are discovering that the old model where the pastor did most of the important tasks him- or herself is increasingly impractical and leads to burnout. A pastor cannot manage a church of over 125 attendees as a sole proprietorship, calling all the shots and checking on all progress. If he or she tries to do so, congregants will be dissatisfied as communication breaks down and the burgeoning tasks of running a church burn out the pastor.

Today, pastors must develop talented teams around themselves. I have discovered that pastors must spend 50–65 percent of their time in team development. Regrettably, most pastors spend 80–85 percent of their time doing the work themselves, with leadership development relegated to 15–20 percent. Though this is laudable, it will not be sufficient to offset the crush of church responsibilities.

Inter-Reliance and Change. We saw in chapter 8 that building consensus and getting reticent congregants on board is one of the most important steps for bringing about change. We saw in chapter 2 that the change process requires not only strategic thinkers, but tactical thinkers and operational leadership; the change process is doomed if only strategic visionaries and operational leaders participate. Inter-reliance and partnership between strategic, tactical, and operational leadership is required to bring about effective change.

An Inter-Reliance To-Do List. Try some of the following exercises to foster inter-reliance among church leaders, both paid and volunteer.

Job Swap. For a short time (a week perhaps), swap jobs. Let the senior pastor do the work of the Generation X pastor, or the church administrator oversee the Sunday schools. The church secretary might want to trade places with an associate pastor, and the worship leader might try his or her hand at the head usher's job. The outcome can be humorous, but insightful. Be sure to tell the congregation you are doing this, for often less than stellar results ensue. Still, I have found congregations appreciate the fact that church leaders are striving to be sensitive to one another, by seeking understanding and appreciation.

Leaders' Retreats. Leaders' retreats are a staple of most churches, but too often they do not take advantage of the off-site environment (a "retreat" means a haven and a departure). Instead of doing more office work at your retreats, use them as a time to share dreams and brainstorm new ideas. Most churches squander the off-site potential of retreat events by simply doing more office work. To workers, retreats often feel more like extended workdays. Resist this temptation, and use your retreats for sharing dreams, focusing on the future, dreaming up new ideas, and deepening your relationships.

Team-Building Exercises. Retreat organizations offer activities designed to promote inter-reliance and team building. So-called rope courses and team-building games can foster reliance through a series of tasks that can only be completed by team effort.[3] In many such courses, tasks are designed to be best completed by the least physically fit or self-confident participant. Thus, in such exercises, even the less athletic and less confident person can contribute significantly. This democratized effort mirrors Paul's statement in 1 Corinthians 12:22–23 (NASB): "On the contrary, it is much truer that the members of the body which seem to be weaker are necessary; and those members of the body which we deem less honorable, on these we bestow more abundant honor."

Leadership Training Programs. Leadership development is critical for ensuring that local leaders grow to the pinnacle of (but not beyond) their leadership abilities. Some churches offer leadership courses on Sunday mornings. Others do so during the week. The purpose is to offer training in all aspects of discipleship and foster church involvement. Many volunteers find it rewarding to take a course and try a new ministry. Plus, the ongoing training in such programs allows volunteers to become acquainted with new opportunities for volunteerism, developing interdepartmental understanding and sharing. Other churches find it helpful to use a congregational human resource department, much like the business model, to host ongoing training and ensure volunteers find appropriate volunteer opportunities.

Organic Leaders Are Connected

An organism is a mutually supportive entity, and thus it is connected at its most basic levels. The organic leader seeks to foster multilayered communication among leaders, as well as between the leaders and the communities they serve.

Connectedness and Leadership. Organic leadership means close relationships are fostered. This does not mean that working relationships alone are fostered, but also that close relationships are fostered in recreation, hobbies, and group activities.

Connectedness and Change. Connectedness is another critical element of the change process. Because change is usually pushing into uncharted, or at least different, cultural waters, those involved must adjust as they go along. Connectedness makes adjustments cohesive.

In chapter 8 we saw that the status quo will usually be unfamiliar with cultural change, and thus they will need to have their questions answered and their concerns heard. Keeping change proponents and the status quo directly connected avoids the disastrous effects of having the pastor become the go-between.

A Connection To-Do List. Church leaders often cringe at the thought of more connectedness with those they serve. "They don't know what they want. Listening to them only gets them and me more confused," confided one irritated pastor. But listening and finding common ground, though messy, is necessary to move a church forward. If reticent congregants do not have a forum to share concerns and feel the leaders have truly heard, they will go underground, only to resurface when some alarm event awakens them to participation. The result will be church polarization.

Thus, church leaders should diligently and repeatedly—even if it becomes laborious—host the following connecting exercises.

Town Hall Meetings. These are important open-invitation meetings to allow congregants and church leaders to interact. Such meetings are publicly announced and should include important topics for the congregation as well as allow questions from the floor on any topic. These meetings will not only allow congregants to stay connected to the leaders and their vision; they will allow leaders to receive firsthand input regarding how their ideas resonate with average congregants.

A Weekly Open-Door Policy. Many organic church leaders have a weekly open-door policy, where anyone can drop by their office without an appointment and spend thirty minutes with the pastor. The thirty-minute rule must be strictly enforced, and if the guest needs more time, a follow-up appointment is scheduled. The purpose of this initial visit is not to diffuse problems (there's not enough time for this) but to make the church leader aware of impending problems before they explode. People who want to habitually attend this open-door time are encouraged to schedule an appointment. This is to ensure that open-door time does not become dominated by a few individuals. The weekly open-door policy emphasizes to the congregation the open nature of the church leadership. This is especially important when a church is undertaking change.

Recreation Activities Together. Often church leaders get to know each other by working alongside one another. However, this can be stifling when their interaction is only work related. It is often advantageous to undertake recreational activities together. This creates an environment where leaders play alongside one another, in hobbies, sports, leisure pursuits, and diversions they mutually enjoy. The key is mutual enjoyment. I once had a pastor who insisted he and I would be better friends if we went fishing together. Fishing had not been enjoyable for me since a friend in my youth unceasingly pestered me about fishing with him. Thus, this pastoral invitation brought up bad memories and held little interest. Out of good intentions, the pastor badgered me for several months, and I seriously questioned if he and I would ever become friends.

Organic Leaders Are Organized

Organization and Leadership. The word *organic* indicates a proper and efficient functioning of many interconnected parts. Thus, an organic organization has a structure and a configuration that is readily understood. Churches should regularly reevaluate their organizational structure and be ready to combine or eliminate committees, programs, and ideas that have outlived their relevance.

However, the organic leader will be cautious to not eliminate organizational elements without heeding the point above: Organic leadership is connected. Thus, the organic leader will work with leaders involved in ineffective or unproductive ministries to create a mutually agreeable plan for appraisal, redirection, or potential cessation. Jesus used a helpful analogy in Luke 13:6–9 when He suggested an unfruitful fig tree be fertilized once more to see if fruit might still be borne upon its limbs. While he was referring to God's graciousness and patience toward unrepentant people, Jesus was also tendering a useful example of how Christians should demonstrate grace and patience. However, this did not mean unending support. Jesus concluded His illustration by saying in verse 9, "If it bears fruit next year, fine; but if not, cut it down."

Organization and Change. It is clear from chapters 6, 7, and 8 that change must be carefully organized. In these chapters we observed that:

- Balancing underlying principles with changing actions consistent with them is a hallmark of the pattern of parenting as well as effectively managing the change process.

189

- Statements of change boundaries (SCBs) can help allay fears that change will go too far or into theologically unacceptable areas.
- The six stages and five triggers of change indicate that change moves in a fairly predictable process toward polarization, unless church leaders carefully organize the change process and change triggers 2 and 4.

An Organization To-do List. In an organic organization church leaders understand how everyone fits together and that there should be little overlap. Thus, in organic organizations most parts of the organization know where they fit, and how they depend on the others. Here are some helpful exercises for fostering organic organizational behavior.

Publish an Organizational Flowchart. Every church above fifty attendees should have a broadly distributed and centrally displayed flowchart that describes all the various activities of the church and how they relate.[4] I have found that for visitors, the church organizational structure ranks in the top five of their most popular questions.[5]

Update Your SCB. Return regularly to chapter 7 to revise, publicize, and announce your SCB to ensure that at the most basic levels you are organized for bringing about unifying change.

Regularly Evaluate Programs and Ministries. Carefully assess each program or ministry's contribution to the organization's long-term goals. But do not end any ministry before gaining board input and compromise. For example, a program may no longer be effective as an evangelistic ministry, yet it may have evolved into a ministry of discipleship for those involved.

Chart Where You Are on the Six Stages of Change. When polarization is evident, go back to chapter 8 if you are headed toward group exit (i.e., on Route A). Stop forward progress toward change and go back and re-legitimize the process. Return to chapter 8 for details on how to reorganize the change process when a congregation is headed toward group exit.

Organic Leaders Are Grassroots Leaders

Grassroots Leadership. Leadership by its nature implies oversight and administration that requires looking at the overall picture. Thus, leadership subtly but persistently raises the leader above loyal church workers in the trenches. To combat this natural distancing, church leaders must make conscientious and continual efforts to go to where their operational leaders work, engage them, and solicit their ideas.

One colleague, Jim Evans, president of a large agricultural manufacturing firm, was legendary for his visits to the factory floor, where he would build connection and consensus with workers there. "He would shove his hands in his pockets and just stand there and listen," recalled Bud, a former employee. "He would listen to you fifteen minutes or longer. It was nice to know he cared about what you were thinking."

Grassroots Change. We saw in chapter 3 that change by its nature is uncommon and uncomfortable for many people. In addition, evangelical churches do not have a good track record in undertaking change. Thus, staying closely connected to those who are implementing change, as well as those who are affected by it, will be critical for operational, tactical, and strategic leaders alike. Unfortunately, many strategic leaders and tactical leaders feel they are too busy to undertake this grassroots connection. However, as we saw in chapters 6, 7 and 8, if you do not stay connected and adjust actions as you implement change, change will appear detached, irrelevant, even antagonistic.

A Grassroots To-Do List. Staying connected to those you serve and ascertaining their needs and their concerns is last but not least in our in study of organic church leadership. This work is similar to the work a missionary must conduct, continually adjusting strategy and tactics based on direct feedback from those one serves. The bane of church leadership is that a gap often emerges between the leader and those they serve.

The church leader might wonder, *Why don't these people come and talk to me?* This is a valid question. However, the church leader does not usually perceive the stature and importance that the average congregant bestows on him or her. Thus when the average person has something to share with the leader, the congregant may unintentionally feel inadequate, inferior, or irrelevant. To thwart this gap, the church leader must intentionally undertake some of the following exercises.

Walk the Halls of Your Church. Compliment people on the jobs they are doing. Greet all people graciously and sincerely. A good way to open conversations is to ask, "How are we doing as an organization?" or "What could we do better?" These questions can help you focus on average congregants who usually do not have a communication conduit to church leadership. This action demonstrates your concern and interest in their opinions (hence this must be a genuine and authentic action, and not synthetically manufactured).

Listen to Church Guests. Churches need newcomer classes and small groups where newcomers can start to fit into the life of the church. Jesus discipled His followers in a small group—the twelve disciples (Matt. 10:1; Luke 6:13)—and since that time small groups have been a hallmark of interconnected organic churches.[6] Thus, provide small get-acquainted groups for newcomers, and visit them regularly. I am often told by pastors that they get their best insights from conversing with newcomers and guests in a relaxed small-group environment.

Listen to Church Workers. Often pastors spend the majority of their time working with the key tactical administrators who help bring to fruition a new idea. However, this creates two degrees of separation between the visionary pastor and the hardworking operational leader. Thus, the strategic visionary should spend regular time with church workers, building relationships and communication.

Listen to Community Leaders. Listening to community leaders will help you ascertain if your church is growing in favor. Acts 2:42 describes four types of church growth. Verses 42–43 describe a growth in maturity. Verses 44–46 add that the church was growing in unity. But the last verse describes two more types of church growth. Verse 47b depicts the church as growing in numbers. (Unfortunately, this is the primary type of growth people think about when they hear the term *church growth*.) Verse 47a contains an important fourth type of growth: growth in "favor of all the people."[7] Referred to as growth in favor, this indicates a church is serving and helping community residents to such a degree that the community, like in New Testament times, is increasingly favorable toward Christians. This is an important type of church growth that we need to recover. If your church is meeting the needs of community residents and helping them encounter Christ, your church should be growing in grassroots favor. Regularly conversing with community leaders, both formally and informally, can help you gauge your community growth in favor.

Observe Community Tuesdays. This idea was suggested by a retired denominational leader in New Orleans. He told me that to stay connected to the community, he religiously observed "Community Tuesdays." This meant he did not go to the office on Tuesday, nor did he do any church work. Rather this minister spent the entire day among community residents. He led a Bible study for migrant workers over lunch, providing a meal. In the afternoon he volunteered for several non-church charities. In the evening he attended community board meetings, a few on which he served and others in which he had interest. The result was that he dedicated eight or more hours each week to being plugged in to the community. As a result, he fostered an awareness of community options, perspectives, and needs.

ORGANIC LEADERS IN A SYNTHETIC WORLD

Organic leadership is not customary, despite the fact that the term *organic* conveys the idea of natural. While organic leadership describes an authentic, genuine leadership style with connectedness and an inter-reliant structure, time usually tries to mutate organic leadership into a prefabricated and disconnected synthetic style.

We must fight this tendency to become distanced from those we serve, especially if we wish to implement appropriate, genuine, and needed change.

Organic change leaders are those who, regardless of gender or skill, make an authentic connection with those they serve and who seek to be relevant and helpful in an increasingly synthetic and impersonal world.

QUESTIONS FOR GROUP STUDY

1. When have your church leaders come together for shared recreation activities?
   - Who fit in and who did not?
   - How might you solicit input for future activities from those who may hesitate to offer their opinions?
2. When was the last time the church leaders attended a retreat?
   - What was the focus of that retreat? Was it church work, or was it getting to know each other better?
   - Which should have been the focus? Why?
3. Do you have a community day during the week?
   - If so, when is it and what do you do?
   - If not, what do you wish you could do? What is keeping you from doing it?
   - Make plans to integrate some variation of a community Tuesday into the regular structure of your week.
4. When was the last time you talked to a guest or newcomer at length?
   - What did the person say could be improved at the church?
   - If you did not ask this or a similar question, what will you ask next time to gauge how the church could better minister to guests and newcomers?
5. Have you noticed a distancing between yourself and the people you serve?
   - How is this distancing manifest?
   - Does it worry you?

- What will you do to stay connected to those you serve?

6. What happened the last time you ended a program or ministry?
   - How was it handled?
   - After reading this book, how would you handle this situation in the future?

7. Which types of church growth do you measure? After each, tell how you measure it. If you do not measure it, how might you do so in the future?
   - growth in maturity (Acts 2:42–43):
   - growth in unity (Acts 2:44–46):
   - growth in favor (Acts 2:47a):
   - growth in number (Acts 2:47b):

NOTES

Chapter 1

1. Change reaction 1 and its probable cause are not summarized beneath the chapter title as are the other change reactions in following chapters, because creating a plan for change is outlined in chapters 3–9 rather than in a single chapter.

2. Several terms describe a church that is dying due to the lack of younger generations. *Old age* describes a church that is dwindling because the community is losing aging residents (C. Peter Wagner, *Your Church Can Be Healthy* [Nashville: Abingdon, 1979], 41–50). This often occurs in rural communities. However, the term *congregational old age* has been used to describe a church whose members are aging, even though there are youthful generations in the community (ibid., 42–43). The closeness of these terms has caused confusion in the church growth movement, and thus the term *geriatrophy* has been adopted as a replacement for the latter term. Geriatrophy is a "combination of the word *geriatric*, meaning the branch of medicine that deals with the diseases of old age, and *atrophy*, denoting a wasting a way or failure to grow" (Bob Whitesel and Kent R. Hunter, *A House Divided: Bridging the Generation Gaps in Your Church* [Nashville: Abingdon, 2001], 31–55).

3. The exact range of generational birth years will be discussed in chapter 2.

4. This research is based on the work of management scholars Bruno Dyck and Frederick A. Starke, who, as laymen, investigated how churches polarize over change. Their research uncovered six stages and five triggers of church change. Their findings are requisite reading for the church leader looking for in-depth analysis into how polarization over change occurs and how to prevent it. (See Bruno Dyck and Frederick A. Starke, "The Formation of Breakaway Organizations: Observations and a Process Model," *Administrative Science Quarterly* (1999), 44:792–822.) In addition, I wrote a book that illustrates the six stages and five triggers of Dyck and Starke with accounts of actual churches: Bob Whitesel, *Staying Power: Why People Leave the Church Over Change and What You Can Do About It* (Nashville: Abingdon, 2003).

5. Dyck and Starke, "The Formation of Breakaway Organizations."

6. C. Peter Wagner says the melting-pot metaphor is an inadequate descriptor for the blending in North America of varying ethnicities and cultures. A melting pot fosters the image of a liquefying of various colorful and tasty ingredients into a grayish unappetizing goo. Wagner suggests a better metaphor for North American culture is that of a stew pot in which each ingredient adds its flavor to the whole, while retaining its unique character (C. Peter Wagner, *Our Kind of People: The Ethical Dimensions of Church Growth in America* [Atlanta: John Knox Press, 1979], 51).

7. A "missional church" reaches out to its community in much the same manner that a missionary might reach out to another culture. It studies the culture of its community, makes contact, explains the good news in their language, and carefully sifts the culture to separate elements that are in opposition to Christ from those that are consistent with Christ's message. (For more on "sifting," see Eddie Gibbs, *I Believe in Church Growth* [Grand Rapids, Mich.: Eerdmans, 1981], 92). For example, missional churches are discovering they can embrace the postmodern emphasis on social ministry to the needy. At the same time the missional church is rejecting elements of the postmodern culture that encourage premarital or extramarital sexual relations. This sorting through the godly and ungodly elements of a culture is what a missionary does daily. In North America this is becoming requisite behavior for evangelical churches as church culture and secular culture become more at variance. See the following two volumes: Darrell L. Guder, ed., *Missional Church: A Vision for the Sending of the Church in North America* (Grand Rapids, Mich.: Eerdmans, 1998) and Ed Stetzer and David Putman, *Breaking the Missional Code: Your Church Can Become a Missionary in Your Community* (Nashville: Broadman & Holman, 2006).

8. In *Staying Power* I explained how the pastor often gets caught in the middle of the ill feelings between change proponents and the status quo, and thus in a majority of cases the pastor quits the church as a result (pp. 114–119).

9. The meaning of the terms *permanence*, *nature*, *will*, and *character* as they relate to God will be investigated in chapters 4 and 5.

10. George G. Hunter III, "Emerging Categories for Understanding Movemental Christianity," address given to the annual meeting of the American Society for Church Growth, Nov. 2005.

11. Emil Brunner, trans. Harold Knight, *The Misunderstanding of the Church* (London: Lutterworth Press, 1952), 15–18.

12. Ibid.

13. Roger Finke and Rodney Stark, "How the Upstart Sects Won America: 1776–1850," *Journal for the Scientific Study of Religion* (1989) 28:27–44; *The Churching of America, 1776–1990: Winners and Losers in Our Religious Economy* (New Brunswick, NJ: Rutgers University Press, 1992).

14. Brunner, *The Misunderstanding of the Church.*

15. Unfortunately, disregard of the change process is only possible for short spans of time. Thus, in congregations where leaders undertake only a short residency, change may sometimes be strategically ignored. Such circumstances would include interim leadership, sabbatical pastorates, and so forth. However, in a majority of circumstances where leaders want to make a positive and long-lasting impact, church change and its various reactions must be addressed and strategized in depth and in advance.

Chapter 2

1. To keep the present discussion from becoming too unwieldy, we will focus on the three broad categories of military leadership theory: strategic leadership, tactical leadership, and operational leadership. For an overview of the historical importance and tensions of the top levels of military leadership, see Mark A. Stoler, *Allies and Adversaries: The Joint Chiefs of Staff, the Grand Alliance, and U.S. Strategy in World War II* (Chapel Hill, NC: University of North Carolina Press, 2000).

2. These are not the only forces that draw pastors into the ministry. However, in my consulting work I have seen these two categories appear with surprising regularity. Additionally, these categories provide a helpful framework for distinguishing how pastors with operational leadership skills vary from those with strategic leadership abilities.

3. Win Arn, "A Church Growth Look at . . . Here's Life America," *The Pastors Church Growth Handbook* (Pasadena, Calif.: Church Growth Press, 1987), 45.

4. There is an important difference in organization theory between theories of *change* and theories of *changing* (see Warren G. Bennis, *Changing Organizations* [New York: McGraw-Hill, 1996]). Theories of change refer to how change occurs, while theories of changing investigate how to control or manipulate

change. Strategic leaders will focus on theories of change, while tactical leaders will gravitate toward theories of changing. Unless this subtle difference is noted, strategic leaders and tactical leaders may be talking about two different things while using the same term. Hence, confusion often results between our visionary leaders and the administrative tactical leaders who must bring these visions to fruition.

5. H. Ozbekhan, "Toward a General Theory of Planning," in E. Jantsch, ed., *Perspective in Planning* (Paris, Organization for Economic Co-operation and Development, 1969), 151.

6. Martin Marty, "Lutheran Scholar Sprinkles Methodist Advice," in *The United Methodist Reporter* (Dallas, Tex.: 1986), March 28.

7. Christian pollster George Barna emphasizes that for a strategic leader, a clear vision of the future is important. Barna, in his book *The Power of Vision* (Ventura, Calif.: Regal, 1992) describes a vision as "a clear mental image of a preferable future imparted by God, and based on an accurate understanding of God, self and circumstances" (28, 38–39). Yet, the popularity of Barna's definition may have clouded the picture, as strategically orientated pastors latched onto this definition, which lacks the complementary emphasis that it is tactical leadership that will get you there.

8. Leith Anderson, *Dying for Change* (Minneapolis, Minn.: Bethany, 1990), 177–178.

9. Phil Miglioratti, "Putting Your Laymen Where They Will Do the Most Good," *The Pastor's Church Growth Handbook* (Pasadena, Calif.: Church Growth Press, 1979), 146.

10. Ibid.

11. Eddie Gibbs, *I Believe in Church Growth* (Grand Rapids, Mich.: Eerdmans, 1981), 380, 383–385.

12. C. Peter Wagner, *Leading Your Church to Growth* (Ventura, Calif.: Regal, 1984), 73–74.

13. John Kotter, *A Force for Change: How Leadership Differs from Management* (Boston: Harvard University Press, 1990).

14. Cited by Wagner, *Leading Your Church to Growth*, 141–165.

15. The architectural analogy is not meant to be wholly precise, but to serve as an approximate illustration. Many architects demonstrate not only strategic big-

ger-picture leadership, but the tactical skills to engineer a building. This is similar to how a church leader may function on several levels of leadership at the same time. Again, the purpose is not to tender an inflexible illustration, but to give a general idea of the complementary interplay of strategic, tactical, and operational skills.

16. Management scholar Russell Ackoff says of tactical leadership, "the principle complexity in planning derives from the interrelatedness of the decisions rather than from the decisions themselves" (Russell L. Ackoff, *A Concept of Corporate Planning* [New York: John Wiley, 1970], 2–3). What Ackoff means is that tactical planning has to take into consideration the connectedness of past, present, and future decisions and work out a complex change strategy that considers all these factors. The most frequent failure in the planning process is due to a lack of tactical leaders who can integrate and coordinate multiple concerns. Often plans for change are brought about by strategic leaders too concerned about the future (to consider fully the present and/or past), and operational leaders who are overly concerned about the needs of the present (and the relationships involved). While in this chapter I have argued all three types of leaders are needed (strategic, tactical, and operational), it is the absence of tactical leaders that often leaves the church with a feeling that change rarely produces good results.

17. Herman R. Van Gunsteren, *The Quest for Control: A Critique of the Rational Control Rule Approach in Public Affairs* (New York: John Wiley, 1976), 2.

18. Ackoff, *A Concept of Corporate Planning*, 1.

19. Miglioratti, "Putting Your Laymen," 146.

20. Ibid.

21. D. Martin Butler and Robert D. Herman, "Effective Ministerial Leadership," *Nonprofit Management and Leadership* (1999), 9:229–239.

22. Gibbs, *I Believe in Church Growth*, 380, 382–383.

23. Kotter, *A Force for Change*. Kotter muddies the water by making an imprecise distinction between leadership and management. Kotter would agree that there are strategic leaders and tactical leaders. However, Kotter calls what strategic leaders do leadership. And he labels what tactical leaders do as management. While it is laudable that Kotter is trying to help distinguish between strategic and tactical leadership, the widespread use of the terms *leadership* and *management* probably means they are too popular to now be more narrowly defined. Thus,

Kotter's goal is good—to distinguish between strategic and tactical leaders—but his terminology is imprecise.

24. Richard G. Hutcheson Jr., *The Wheel Within the Wheel: Confronting the Management Crisis of the Pluralistic Church* (Atlanta: John Knox Press, 1979), 54.

25. Gary Yukl, *Managerial Practices Survey* (Albany, NY: Gary Yukl and Man Associates, 1990).

26. Cited by Wagner, *Leading Your Church to Growth*, 141–165.

27. Margaret Mead, http://www.quoteworld.org/quotes/8891.

28. Miglioratti, "Putting Your Laymen," 146.

29. Ibid.

30. Ibid.

31. Gibbs, *I Believe in Church Growth*, 380–381.

32. Miglioratti, "Putting Your Laymen," 147.

33. Though today tactical leaders are often missing in our churches, this was not always the case. In the early 1980s Peter Wagner and other leaders in the church growth movement lamented that mostly tactical leaders were being trained in seminaries. Wagner would label strategic leadership as *strong leadership,* and tactical leadership he would call *enabler leadership.* He observed in 1984, with obvious Orwellian overtones, "one reason why strong pastoral leadership is not characteristic of many of America's churches is that in the recent past clergy have been taught just the opposite in the seminaries . . . . They were taught to reject strong, authoritative, directive pastoral leadership . . . . The alternative has been the model of pastor as an 'enabler'" (Wagner, *Leading Your Church to Growth*, 73–75). What exactly is an enabler? Richard Hutcheson puts it this way: "An enabler or facilitator is a relatively uninvolved technician who understands the process by which things are accomplished and who enables other to achieve goals' (Hutcheson, *The Wheel Within the Wheel*, 54)." What Wagner and Hutcheson are describing as enablers, I would define in organizational terms as tactical leaders. And I would disagree with Hutcheson on one point. I have found that tactical leaders are not "relatively uninvolved," but only appear to be so because they enjoy the impersonal and technical tasks of planning, analysis, evaluation, and adjustment.

34. Hutcheson, in *The Wheel Within the Wheel* (53), describes how the group

dynamics movement within the human resource field emphasized interpersonal relationships in management. Thus, tactical leadership came to be viewed incorrectly as more profane in contrast to its strategic and operational counterparts. However, the reader of this chapter should be able to see that all three leadership skills—strategic, tactical, and operational—are required for effective change to take place.

35. The 12 percent of the strategic leaders who are unengaged is probably due to the lack of tactical leaders, as well. Church leaders often lament that there is no one in the church available to implement their new ideas, and thus they keep their ideas to themselves.

36. This questionnaire is not designed to be a definitive categorization for these three types of leadership skills, but a general indicator. You may find you scored differently than you anticipated. In such circumstances and if you feel comfortable doing so, share with friends and coworkers your score and ask for comment on your leadership categorization. Remember, neither category is superior to the others; the proper and organic functioning of all three is required for change to take place. In addition, often leaders move from one leadership category to another based on circumstance or time. For instance, sometimes congregants who have been tactical leaders in the past and know the great degree of energy and effort such leadership requires may want a sabbatical from tactical duties. This is permissible and proper, since God himself rested from His labors (Gen. 2:3) and required this of His children (Ex. 20:8; Lev. 25:2).

Chapter 3

1. Here and throughout this book, I will use the customary congregational size designations as codified by Gary McIntosh in *One Size Doesn't Fit All: Bringing Out the Best in Any Size Church* (Grand Rapids, Mich.: Revell, 1999), 17–19. These church attendance categories include the following:

Small, 15–200 attendees, relational in orientation

Midsized, 201–400 attendees, programmatic in orientation

Large, 401+, organizational in orientation

2. The 2001 census in the United Kingdom created controversy when it listed the following ethnicities. These categories are reprinted here again, not to offend, but to demonstrate the broad range of possible designations and the difficulty in

creating acceptable lists. Thus, the purpose of this list is simply to acquaint the reader with the immense variety (and potential controversy) of ethnic groupings.

White: British, White; Irish, White; Other

Mixed: White and Black Caribbean, Mixed; White and Black African, Mixed; White and Asian, Mixed; Other

Asian: Indian, Asian; Sri Lankan, Asian; Pakistani, Asian; Bangladeshi, Asian; Other

Black or Black British: Black Caribbean, Black or Black British; Black African, Black or Black British; Other

Chinese or Other: Chinese, Chinese or Other; Other

3. *The World Factbook: CIA Edition* (Washington, D.C.: Potomac Books; rev. ed., 2006, CIA 2005 ed.).

4. For the reader looking for a more in-depth analysis of socioeconomic levels and their influence on behavior, consult David Jaffee's books: *Levels of Socioeconomic Development Theory* (New York: Praeger, 1998), and *Organization Theory* (New York: McGraw-Hill, 2001).

5. Immanuel Wallerstein, *The Modern World-System I: Capitalist Agriculture and the Origins of the European World-Economy in the Sixteenth Century, Studies in Social Discontinuity* (Burlington, Mass.: Academic Press, 1980).

6. Joseph V. Hickey and William E. Thompson, *Society in Focus: An Introduction to Sociology*, 5th ed. (Boston, Mass.: Allyn & Bacon, 2004).

7. See Bob Whitesel and Kent R. Hunter, *A House Divided: Bridging the Generation Gaps in Your Church* (Nashville: Abingdon, 2001).

8. For an extensive analysis on the distinguishing characteristics of each generation see Whitesel and Hunter, *A House Divided* and Gary McIntosh, *One Church, Four Generations: Understanding and Reaching All Ages in Your Church* (Grand Rapids, Mich.: Baker, 2002).

9. Bob Whitesel, *Inside the Organic Church: Learning From 12 Emerging Congregations* (Nashville: Abingdon, 2006), x–xii.

10. Mike Yankoski, *Under the Overpass: A Journey of Faith on the Streets of America* (Colorado Springs: Multnomah, 2005).

11. Whitesel, *Inside the Organic Church*, x–xii, xxviii–xxxiii. For a detailed look at the postmodern Xers' fresh ideas for the church, as well as the differences between modernism and postmodernism, see *Inside the Organic Church: Learning From 12*

Emerging Congregations, pp. x–xii, xxviii–xxxiii.

12. Anonymous, *Thunder Roads Magazine*, vol. 5, no. 2 (2007): 5.

13. For more on this innovative, growing evangelical church with the unlikely name, see the chapter dedicated to the church and what every church can learn in Whitesel, *Inside the Organic Church*, 76–87.

14. Paul Hiebert, *Cultural Anthropology* (Grand Rapids, Mich.: Baker, 1976), 25.

15. The Beatles, *Sergeant Pepper's Lonely Heart's Club Band*, (London: Parlophone Records, 1967).

16. John Mayer, *Continuum*, (New York: Sony Records, 2006).

17. Quoted in Arthur Johnston, *The Battle for World Evangelism* (Wheaton, Ill.: Tyndale, 1978), 138.

18. Charles Kraft, *Christianity in Culture: A Study of Dynamic Biblical Theologizing in Cross-Cultural Perspective* (Maryknoll, NY: Orbis Books, 1979), 113.

19. Ibid.

20. Ibid., 114.

21. Eddie Gibbs, *I Believe in Church Growth* (Grand Rapids, Mich.: Eerdmans, 1981), 92.

22. Kraft, *Christianity in Culture*, 148.

23. Sherwood Eliot Wirt, *The Social Conscience of the Evangelical* (New York: Harper & Row, 1968), 50.

24. If you are unsure of how to accomplish this, ask someone in your congregation who is under age twenty-five to help you.

25. Herein lies a caveat for multiple-site churches. A recent spate of attention has been garnered by these adaptive congregations (see Bill Easum and Dale Travis, *Beyond the Box: Innovative Churches That Work* [Loveland, Colo.: Group, 2003]). However, too often in these churches the tactic of using multiple locations is emphasized over the more organizationally important understanding of the cultures that different locations reach. To ensure the location or a resultant colonization by the mother church do not become the goals, these churches are better organizationally described and managed as multicultural churches.

26. Chapter 1 (pp. 1-12) of *Inside the Organic Church* describes this unique congregation and their clustering of small groups to create over thirty sub-con-

gregations where discipleship and teaching is fostered in this burgeoning mega-church. See also Bob Whitesel, "The Perfect Cluster: For Young Adults, St. Tom's, Sheffield Creates Extended Families, And Everyone Knows Where They Fit," *Outreach Magazine* (Vista, Calif.: Outreach Publishing, 2005), May/June, 112–114.

27. It can be seen from the above discussion that these are oversimplifications. But because significant conflict has erupted over such generalizations, it is important their conflicting perspectives be considered and addressed in an effective church change strategy.

28. C. Peter Wagner and others have scrutinized the Homogeneous Unit Principle (HUP), which suggests that people like to become Christians without crossing cultural barriers (C. Peter Wagner, *Our Kind of People: the Ethical Dimensions of Church Growth in America* [Atlanta: John Knox Press, 1979], 110–123; Ralph H. Elliott, *Church Growth That Counts* [Valley Forge, Penn.: Judson Press, 1982], 55–63;). Research bears this out (Charles Arn, *How to Start a New Service: Your Church Can Reach New People* [Grand Rapids, Mich.: Baker, 1997], 23–31). However, there are some churches that thrive as multiethnic churches offering only multiethnic worship experiences. Wagner argues that such a church is also a homogeneous unit, only that it is predominately a homogeneous unit of people who enjoy multiethnic aesthetics. This makes sense to me, for I would count myself among them. However, in my two decades as a church growth consultant I have found people like myself who enjoy this every week to be the exception rather than the rule.

29. Whitesel and Hunter, *A House Divided*, 25–30.

30. George G. Hunter III, *The Contagious Congregation: Frontiers in Evangelism and Church Growth* (Nashville: Abingdon, 1979), 63.

31. Arn, *How to Start a New Service*, 23–31.

32. Daniel Sanchez, "Viable Models for Churches in Communities Experiencing Ethnic Transition" (Pasadena, Calif.: Fuller Theological Seminary, 1976), paper; and Wagner, *Our Kind of People*, 159–163.

Chapter 4

1. This case study can be generalized in only a limited way because the sample used is client churches. Because these churches have sought me out as a

church growth consultant, most congregations tend to be strongly to moderately evangelical and are facing a long-term planning crisis. Thus, while the categories that emerge from their responses are helpful for noting a general overview of congregational strengths, these results should not be applied uncritically. Rather, these categories and their rank result from a research base that includes churches facing concern over the future, and who embrace an evangelical theology. If this mirrors your congregation, these categories and their rankings may be valid for you. However in this discussion my purpose has not been to create a widely applicable list of church strengths, but to highlight that congregants usually perceive church strengths to be underlying and enduring in nature, will, and character attributes, rather than specific ministries or programs.

2. The results here refer to the general caring personality and kindly disposition of a church. Specific targets of that care are categorized separately and occur farther down the list.

3. Students of church organizational behavior may want to investigate these results. The ranking of these categories and their prevalence can tell us a great deal about the mindsets and priorities of evangelical churches undergoing uncertainty about long-term planning.

4. Note that these are perceived strengths from the viewpoints of church leaders. This does not mean these may be strengths to visitors or those outside leadership. I have visited many churches who rated friendliness near the top, only to find newcomers and guests would have rated their friendliness factor much lower.

5. The layperson mobilization movement in the 1960s and 1970s was designed to get laypeople more involved in leading churches. A side benefit has been that it has forced the laity to theologize, to grapple with what the Bible says about a variety of topics.

6. Roger Finke and Rodney Stark, "How the Upstart Sects Won America: 1776–1850," in *The Journal for the Scientific Study of Religion* (1989, 28:27–44); and *The Churching of America: Winners and Losers in Our Religious Economy* (New Brunswick, NJ: Rutgers University Press, 1992).

7. Harvey Cox, "What Ever Happened To Theology?" in *Christianity in Crisis* (1975), 35:114–115.

8. Millard Erickson, "God and Change" in *Southern Baptist Journal of Theology*, 1, 2, (1997), 38. Erickson expands this article in his book *God the*

Father Almighty: A Contemporary Exploration of the Divine Attributes (Grand Rapids, Mich.: Baker, 2003).

9. Due to the words' growing popularity, we shall refer to *immutable* and *mutable*, yet to a measured degree. The purpose here is not to confuse the volunteer church person with unfamiliar terms, but rather to help everyone understand terms that have broad and useful meanings.

10. Millard Erickson, "God and Change," 38.

11. In philosophy this is called the *teleological* argument for God's existence. This means that because we see the design of God's creation (the Greek word *teleos* means design or purpose), these results should be testimony to the fact that God exists and persists. Thus, we know God exists because we see the results of His creation. And, we know He persists because we witness that He continues to care, direct, and orchestrate creation. This was best articulated by St. Thomas Aquinas as his fifth way (or proof) of God's existence. See Saint Thomas Aquinas, *Summa Theologiae*, Pt. 1, Qu. 2, Art. 3, in *Basic Writings of Saint Thomas Aquinas*, ed. Anton C. Pegis (New York: Random, 1945), I.

12. Amos Hakham, *The Bible: Psalms with the Jerusalem Commentary*, vol. 3 (New York: Judaica Press, 2003), 21.

13. Ibid.

14. Pieter A. Verhoef, *The Books of Haggai and Malachi* (Grand Rapids, Mich.: Eerdmans, 1987), 299.

15. Martin Dibelius, trans. Michael A. Williams, *A Commentary on the Epistle of James* (Philadelphia: Fortress Press, 1976), 99.

16. Peter H. Davids, *The Epistle of James: A Commentary on the Greek Text* (Grand Rapids, Mich.: Eerdmans, 1982), 86.

17. Dibelius, *A Commentary on the Epistle of James*, 104; and E. S. Fiorenza, *The Interpreter's Dictionary of the Bible*, Supplementary Volume (Nashville: Abingdon, 1976), 337.

18. Millard Erickson, "God and Change," 39.

19. The attributes of God are so expansive and intensive in nature, will, and character that only a few examples will be given and those for comparison purposes only.

20. The passages cited in this chapter largely ignore methodology. Though general categories of methodology may be mentioned (such as creating, tithing,

offerings, new birth), the exact mechanics of each are not discussed. This is because the focus of each of these passages is that God does not change in His underlying permanence, nature, will, and character.

21. Today some theologians embrace a variation of process theology, holding that God is changing in His essence, in His basic, underlying characteristics. This author and others (Erickson, 50) believe their viewpoint is influenced more by modern and postmodern suppositions than by scriptural accuracy. The three passages discussed in this chapter would clearly argue against any idea that God would change in His essential nature, will, and character.

22. An extended examination of immutability is beyond this short book. My purpose here is to provide church leaders, both lay and clergy, with a short overview and rationale for the immutability of God's underlying permanence, nature, will, and character. The reader who wishes a more detailed and rousing look at this topic should consult the following volumes:

Wayne Gruden, *Systematic Theology* (Grand Rapids, Mich.: Zondervan, 1994), 163–168.

Joseph Hallman, "The Mutability of God: Tertullian to Lactantius," *Theological Studies* (1981) 42, 373–93.

Carl F. H. Henry, *God, Revelation and Authority*, vol. 5 (Waco, Tex.: Word, 1982), 286–294.

Chapter 5

1. I have written extensively on the polarization that arises over change and how to diffuse it in *Staying Power: Why People Leave the Church Over Change and What You Can Do About It* (Nashville: Abingdon, 2003). In this book I describe how change takes place through a six-stage and five-trigger process. I will also discuss this further in chapter 8, because it is critical that church leaders understand the forces and stages that give rise to tensions and polarization over change. For an in-depth analysis of how change creates polarization and how to overcome it, read *Staying Power.*

2. Millard Erickson, "God and Change" in *Southern Baptist Journal of Theology*, 1, 2, (1997), 41–42.

3. Ibid., 42.

4. Type-4 change does not apply to God for the same reasons type-1 does not.

5. The theological terms for God's attributes as all knowing and all powerful are *omniscience* and *omnipotence* respectively.

6. Erickson, "God and Change," 42.

7. Ibid.

8. Erickson lists ten types of change in the Bible (pp. 41–42). While these ten types are valid, they do not all bear upon the present discussion. However, the reader wishing a fuller discussion should consult Erickson's book *God the Father Almighty: A Contemporary Exploration of the Divine Attributes* (Grand Rapids, Mich.: Baker, 2003). To avoid confusing the reader and to keep the discussion from becoming too unwieldy, I have pared down Erickson's list and renumbered it in a more uniform manner.

9. Jesus' five parables on overcoming the relational change when salvation is involved are:

The parable of the lost sheep (Luke 15:3–7)

The parable of the lost coin (Luke 15:8–10)

The parable of the loving father (Luke 15:11–32)

The parable of the shrewd manager (Luke 16:1–18)

The parable of the rich man and the beggar (Luke 16:19–31)

10. Erickson, *God and Change*, 42.

11. *Life Application Study Bible* (Wheaton, Ill.: Tyndale House, 1991), commentary on Leviticus 11:47.

12. Norman Geisler, "Alleged Errors in the Bible—Part Four," *Encyclopedia of Christian Apologetics* (Grand Rapids, Mich.: Baker, 1999).

13. Some commentators debate if this passage was contained in the original writing, since the earliest manuscripts end at verse 8. Whether this is the case is beyond this present discussion. However, at the least, this passage attests to the types of miracles that were occurring in the early church.

14. J. Rodman Williams, *10 Teachings* (Carol Stream, Ill.: Creation House, 1974), 17.

15. Albert and Loy Morehead, eds. *The New American College Dictionary* (New York: Signet, 1995).

16. Erickson, "God and Change," 43.

17. Ibid.

18. Morehead, *The New American College Dictionary*.

19. Francis Brown, S. R. Brown, and Charles A. Briggs, *The Brown, Driver, Briggs Hebrew and English Lexicon* (Peabody, Mass.: Hendrickson, 1996).

20. Richard Rice, "Biblical Support for a New Perspective," in Clark Pinnock, Richard Rice, John Sanders, William Hasker, and David Basinger, *The Openness of God: A Biblical Challenge to the Traditional Understanding of God* (Downers Grove, Ill.: InterVarsity, 1994). Here Rice analyzes more than forty passages that describe God as repenting. Erickson uncovers a few more such passages ("God and Change," 45–46) and in turn analyzes them. The student interested in a thorough investigation into the passages that declare God repents will want to consult this book and article.

21. Erickson, "God and Change," 44.

22. Franz Laubach, "*metamelomai*," *The New International Dictionary of New Testament Theology*, Colin Brown, ed., translated from *Theologisches Begriffslexikon Zum Neuen Testament*, eds. Lothar Coenen, Erich Beyreuther, and Hans Bietenhard (Grand Rapids, Mich.: Zondervan, 1967), 356.

23. Michael D. Ryan in *The Contemporary Explosion of Theology* (Metuchen, NJ: Scarecrow Press, 1975) points out that many people today have preconceived appreciation for or aversion to the concept of regret and genuine repentance. He points out that though the meaning of repenting or turning from one's sins is foundational and key, we can begin discussion with non-churched people by substituting the phrase *consciousness change* for the word *repent* in our initial conversations with them. Ryan points out that *consciousness change* is a widely used term among secular intellectuals to describe a change in mind that affects one's entire life. In other words, what former Vice President Al Gore is doing by promoting his movie on global warming is to foster *consciousness change* in moviegoers. His purpose is to change people in all areas of their life. Charles A. Reich, in his book *The Greening of America* ([New York: Random, 1970], 299–348), popularized *consciousness change,* and it has gained popularity with secular audiences. To help such audiences understand what repentance and a turning from one's sins means, we may want to begin by stating that Jesus wants a *consciousness change* meaning a change in one's entire being, outlook, and direction with an accompanying regret for one's old direction. While Gore's attempt at *consciousness change* regarding global warming is important and laudable, it pales in comparison to humankind's need for *consciousness change* in their attitude

toward their sins and the salvation that only Jesus can offer.

24. *Cainotophobia* means an abnormal fear of newness, and comes from combining two Greek words: *kainos*, meaning new; and *phobia*, meaning fear. Cainotophobia is sometimes confused with misoneism, which means a fear of change or innovation, and comes from combining the Greek words *miso-* (dislike or fear) with *neos* (new) (*The American Heritage Dictionary of the English Language*, 4th ed. [Boston: Houghton Mifflin, 2000]). *Cainotophobia* is a fear of the newness that results from change. While the two are similar, *cainotophobia* has to do more with a fear of the change results, while *misoneism* has to do with a fear of the change process itself. Thus both words would be valid for the reticence we experience in our churches. However, while the Church may suffer from both maladies, it is primarily cainotophobia that prevents churches from tackling change due to a fear of change reactions.

25. See stages 4 and 5 in the Process Model for Change and Group Exit in Bob Whitesel, *Staying Power: Why People Leave the Church Over Change and What You Can Do About It* (Nashville: Abingdon, 2003).

26. Jung Young Lee likens this understanding of change to the outlook in Eastern thought of *yin* (rest) and *yang* (movement) as part of all creation. Jung Young Lee, *The Theology of Change: A Christian Concept of God in an Eastern Perspective* (Markynoll, NY: Orbis, 1979).

Chapter 6

1. Some commentators point out that the Greek word for *give us birth* can carry both the emphasis of male procreation and female birth. However, the straightforwardness of the term as an image of birthing persuades me to include it here as a characteristic of motherhood.

2. Historically, the fatherhood of God has received greater attention than His motherly attributes. This may be due to the patriarchal influences of Greek and similar cultures. For an overview regarding how the emphasis of God's fatherhood took precedence, see Peter Widdicombe, *The Fatherhood of God from Origen to Athanasius* (Oxford: Clarendon, 2000).

3. Mark could have translated this from the Aramaic *abba* into a more widely understood Greek word. However, he left this expression of Jesus intact. The rationale can be that it was widely understood and needed no translation. But it

could be because Mark felt this term of endearment was so poignant and power-ful that it was best to leave it in Aramaic baby-gibberish to emphasize the trust-ing, personal, and cherished relationship that exists between the Son of God and the Father, and that should be mirrored in His offspring.

4. Otfried Hofius, *abba* in *The New International Dictionary of New Testament Theology*, Colin Brown, ed., translated from *Theologisches Begriffslexikon Zum Neuen Testament*, eds. Lothar Coenen, Erich Beyreuther, and Hans Bietenhard (Grand Rapids, Mich.: Zondervan, 1967), 614.

5. Alister E. McGrath, *Christian Theology: An Introduction*, Third ed. (Oxford: Blackwell, 2001), 266.

6. Sallie McFaque, *Models of God: Theology for an Ecological Nuclear Age* (Philadelphia: Fortress, 1987), 122–123.

7. Note the prominent use of the male terms *He* and *Him*.

8. Hans Kung makes an important distinction between the biblical model of a loving God and what adversaries to Christianity often misperceive. Kung writes, "This Father God is nothing like the God feared by Marx, Nietzsche and Freud, terrifying men from childhood onward into feelings of anxiety and guilt, con-stantly moralizingly pursing him: a God who is in fact only the projection of instilled fears, of human domination, lust for power, arrogance and vindictive-ness." Hans Kung, *On Being a Christian* (London, Collins: 1977), 312.

9. John W. Miller, *Calling God "Father": Essays on the Bible, Fatherhood and Culture* (New York: Paulist, 1999), 93.

10. Widdicombe, *The Fatherhood of God*, 614.

11. I. Howard Marshall, *New Testament Theology: Many Witnesses, One Gospel* (Downers Grove, Ill.: InterVarsity, 2004), 192.

Chapter 7

1. Today there is confusion and tension over different styles of worship, with several names employed. To help clear up some of this confusion, I have created consistent terminology in my books, categorizing worship celebrations into the following broad categories.

Traditional Worship. This is a worship celebration characterized by tradi-tional hymns, liturgy, structure, and aesthetics. Some churches call this *classical* worship. This style appeals primarily to worshippers who have grown up in the church or have a long history with it and thus appreciate conventional and time-honored structures. Constancy and predictability are often valued by older congregants, because as they age they encounter uncertainty in their financial, health, and relational lives. As a result, they may need and enjoy a constancy in church worship. Traditional worship is comfortable and familiar, and can help them weather the uncertainties of aging. In *A House Divided: Bridging the Generation Gaps in Your Church* (Nashville, Abingdon: 2001), Kent Hunter and I point out that churches must not sacrifice on the altar of expediency the traditional worship expressions that meet the needs of aging congregants seeking constancy.

Modern Worship. Many people refer to this style as *contemporary* worship, yet this word does not clearly describe the style. Contemporary means "of the latest style or fashion," and much of the contemporary worship music has shades of 1970s country or folk rock. Millions of Christians have come to enjoy modern worship. However, when an unchurched person enters our churches expecting contemporary music and encounters music reminiscent of an earlier era, the unchurched person may think congregants at best naïve and at worst deceptive. Thus, there is no need to propagate a term that has a confusing meaning. Instead, the term *modern* might be a more befitting descriptor. The modern era, which began with the Enlightenment and extends to some degree today, is the realm of the baby boomers (for more on the modern era and the postmodern era, see chapter 3 as well as Bob Whitesel, *Inside the Organic Church: Learning from 12 Emerging Congregations* [Nashville: Abingdon, 2006]). Thus, modern worship is probably a good description of music influenced by the Boomer Generation's historical roots. But the title matters little, except to convey an understanding of the musical genre being described. Thus, to parallel the postmodern music I shall describe shortly, and to foster consistency, I will refer to what many call contemporary music with the more precise designation: modern music.

Blended Worship. In their attempts to move from traditional worship to modern worship and attract the boomers, many churches have blended or combined their traditional worship and modern worship into "blended worship." They may not be large enough to host separate traditional and modern worship expressions. To address this concern, Kent Hunter, Charles Arn, and I have written elsewhere how churches as small as 75 in attendance can move into parallel traditional and modern worship services (see Whitesel and Hunter, *A House Divided*, especially chapter 8: "Worship in a Tri-generational Format" and Charles Arn, *How to Start a Second Service: Your Church Can Reach New People*, Grand Rapids, Mich.: Baker, 1997). On the other hand, churches who could host two different styles of worship often blend their services because congregants want to see each other and stay connected. Charles Arn (ibid.) points out that when a church offers fewer worship options, evangelism suffers. I have observed that blended services cause significant conflict among attendees. It seems that as soon as one style begins to worship—let's say for example the builders are enjoying a rousing hymn—the flow is interrupted by a song from a different culture, for example a contemporary chorus. "Hootenanny songs" is how one disgruntled builder put it. Having married a Lutheran (from the old Norwegian Synod), I often kid my wife that she acts like anything written after the time of Johann Sebastian Bach and Martin Luther is rock music (which would include all Charles Wesley's great hymns). My wife and I have come to better understand each other's genres of music, and a mutual admiration and appreciation of musical styles has resulted. But to people new to Christianity, the blended format may seem too much of an artistic hodgepodge to be attractive. This is especially true because in the secular world musical styles are separated on the radio, with classical music reminiscent of traditional church music one of the least popular genres. But as mentioned earlier, older members might like, and need, the continuity and stability of a traditional style of worship music. Thus, both genres are needed. But our blending the two into one worship celebration usually has limited success. Blended worship has just about enough of everything to make just about everyone mad. Leaders of congregations employing blended services usually give this comment a stirring chorus of affirmations and knowing glances.

Postmodern Worship. This is worship largely instigated and led by postmodern Gen-Xers. This group has sought to create a more authentic, genuine, interconnected, and heartfelt worship expression. Believing boomer worship too often morphs into production, professionalism, and perfection, postmodern Xers seek a more organic, natural, less precise, but more engaging worship. These Xers see encounter with God as more important than structure or style; they welcome flexibility, improvisation, and artistic variation. I have profiled twelve of these churches in my book *Inside the Organic Church*. Christian Xers welcome all artists, often encouraging participation from painters, sculptors, actors, dancers, and artists of all mediums. As a result postmodern worship often has interactive stations, similar to Stations of the Cross, ringing the worship space. These often include community art stations, which attendees are encouraged to visit during worship and to contribute to a community art project that represents the mood and atmosphere of the worship. I have described in *Inside the Organic Church* dozens of examples and contact information for postmodern Xers who are reinventing worship for the better. In fact, I have called these expressions *organic churches* because they embrace a holistic approach to the arts, as well as connectedness with each other and to their mission field.

2. If a church does not belong to a denomination, it is helpful to consult the statement of faith of a comparable church and its denomination. The purpose of this exercise is to ensure in even new or nonaffiliated churches an awareness of historical creeds and vital elements of orthodoxy.

3. Saying a local congregation has unique giftings does not indicate these giftings are limited to one congregation. By *unique* giftings I mean those congregational strengths the Holy Spirit has empowered the congregation to contribute to the local ministry matrix. As such, these giftings will be noticed by people outside the congregation as well as within the congregation as unique gifts of this congregation from the Lord to the community.

4. Unique giftings that churches may possess are sometimes called *core competencies:* skills and attributes in which a church is uniquely gifted—those things an organization does well—and which are recognized as such by the church and the community. Core competencies possess four traits: they are valuable, rare, costly to imitate, and non-substitutable. Another way to say this is that "core competencies distinguish a company competitively and reflect its personality" (Michael A. Hitt, R. Duane Ireland, and Robert E. Hoskisson, *Strategic Management: Competitiveness and Globalization*, 4th ed. [Cincinnati, Ohio: South-Western College Publishing, 2001], 113).

5. For information about Stephen Ministries, visit their Web site: www.stephenministries.org.

6. www.stephenministries.org/stephenministry, 2007. A fuller definition is, "in Stephen Ministry congregations, lay caregivers (called Stephen Ministers) provide one-to-one Christian care to the bereaved, hospitalized, terminally ill, separated, divorced, unemployed, relocated, and others facing a crisis or life chal-

lenge. Stephen Ministry helps pastors and congregations provide quality caring ministry for as long as people need it" ("Introduction to Stephen Ministry," www.stephenministries.org/stephenministry, 2007).

7. *Stakeholder* is another term borrowed from Old West parlance, where miners would hammer a wooden stake in a riverbed to signify that the area downstream was their property. This practice came to be known as "staking your claim." Thus, a stakeholder is a person who has a claim upon the church and its future.

8. In an earlier book, *Growth by Accident, Death by Planning: How Not to Kill a Growing Congregation* (Nashville: Abingdon, 2004), I showed how lack of evaluation was one of the eleven most prevalent mistakes to which church leaders succumb, and which stunts church growth. For more information and creative ideas regarding how to facilitate ongoing evaluation, see chapter 7: "Missteps with Evaluation" in *Growth by Accident*, 97–107.

Chapter 8

1. Bob Whitesel, *Staying Power: Why People Leave The Church Over Change* (Abingdon Press, 2003). This book takes an in-depth look at each of the six-stages and five-triggers of the change process. I devote a chapter to each stage or trigger, while using actual church case studies to illustrate each. For the church currently or formerly embroiled in polarization over change, this book can provide insights and tools to bring about change in a unifying, cohesive manner.

2. See Bruno Dyck, and Frederick A. Starke, The Formation of Breakaway Organizations: Observations and a Process Model, *Administrative Science Quarterly* (1999) 44:792-822; and Frederick A. Starke and Bruno Dyck, "Upheavals in Congregations: The Causes and Outcomes of Splits," in *Review of Religious Research* (1996) 38:159-174.

3. For more on corporate costs associated with losing change proponents, see Andrea Butter and David Pogue, *Piloting Palm: The Inside Story of Palm, Handspring and the Birth of the Billion Dollar Handheld Industry* (Hoboken, New Jersey: Wiley, 2002).

4. Bruno Dyck, and Frederick A. Starke, "The Formation of Breakaway Organizations: Observations and a Process Model," op. cit., 44:792-822.

5. This negative legitimizing often happens when a newcomer is thrust into a

leadership role. For instance, when a new pastor is hired and the church is polarized, status quo and change proponents will both seek out the new leader to politic for their respective causes. If the new leader is unacquainted with the change process, and inadvertently *negatively legitimizes* either faction, the church is headed toward another spiral of polarization and group exit.

6. Frederick A. Starke and Bruno Dyck. "Upheavals in Congregations: The Causes and Outcomes of Splits," op. cit., 38:159-174.

7. Bruno Dyck, and Frederick A. Starke, "The Formation of Breakaway Organizations."

8. Ibid.

9. C. Peter Wagner, *Our Kind of People: The Ethical Dimensions of Church Growth in America* (Atlanta: John Knox Press, 1979), p. 51. Wagner also makes a good point that the popular postmodern term "mosaic" does not effectively convey a pluralism of cultures, for the "pieces of a mosaic barely touch each other and do not interact," ibid.

10. Remember, that compromise is in methodology only, not in the congregation's underlying nature, will, or characteristics. The harmonizing event seeks to foster compromise behavior, but this is only in tactics and not in the biblical, historical or congregational values and boundaries that your SCB describes.

11. Listening to varied voices is an important component in fostering creativity. For examples of churches using a wide-range of voices to stimulate creatively or to discover ten steps for increasing creative capital see respectively: Bob Whitesel, *Inside the Organic Church*, op cit., "Figure 9: A Comparisons Between Institutionalization and Improvisation," pp. 119-120, and *Growth by Accident, Death By Planning*, op. cit., "Missteps With Innovation: Instead of Entrepreneur – Innovator!" pp. 89-93.

Chapter 9

1. Mike Yankoski, *Under the Overpass: A Journey of Faith on the Streets of America* (Colorado Springs: Multnomah, 2005).

2. I use the term *head knowledge* to indicate a modern-era propensity to emphasize secondary research and study (for example, reading books, journal articles, and so forth). Secondary research is based on published or collected data. Primary research, on the other hand, is conducted by the person him- or herself.

Subsequently, the firsthand experience of primary research usually leads to more insight for the researcher. Pimary research is usually valued more than secondary research. Postmodern Xers may intuitively understand this, and tend to shun secondary research (reading a book or article) in favor of primary research (experiencing it themselves). They value personal experience and deep-rooted insights that come from conducting their own research. Therefore, when I use the term *head knowledge*, I am referring to knowledge that emerges from secondary research. When I use *experience* I am referring to firsthand knowledge gained from primary research. I have chosen not to employ the terms *primary* and *secondary research* in the body of this chapter to avoid confusing the casual reader. However, here this added explanation may help the academic reader understand my nuances in contrasting head knowledge with experience. For more on primary and secondary research and their distinctives, see Louis E. Boone and David L. Kurtz, *Contemporary Marketing*, 11th ed. (Manson, Ohio: Thomson South-Western, 2004), 200–210.

3. For examples of seminaries that are striving to balance theoretical knowledge with practical experience, see my interviews with five seminary leaders in chapter 9: "Missteps with Staff Education" in *Growth By Accident, Death By Planning: How Not to Kill a Growing Congregation* (Nashville: Abingdon, 2004), 121–131.

4. Emil Brunner, trans. Harold Knight, *The Misunderstanding of the Church*, (London: Lutterworth, 1952), 15–18.

5. Roger Finke and Rodney Stark, *The Churching of America, 1776–1990: Winners and Losers in Our Religious Economy* (New Brunswick, NJ: Rutgers University Press, 1992), 154–166. While Finke and Stark are emphasizing the role of conformity and other factors in ministerial education, their narrative also implies a negative effect from trial-and-error pastoral education.

6. Brunner, *The Misunderstanding of the Church*, 15–18; Roger Finke and Rodney Stark, "How the Upstart Sects Won America: 1776–1850," *Journal for the Scientific Study of Religion* (1989) 28:27–44; *The Churching of America*.

7. Bruno Dyck and Frederick A. Starke, "The Formation of Breakaway Organizations: Observations and a Process Model," *Administrative Science Quarterly* (1999), 44:792–822.

8. Pastors will be less overwhelmed by the tasks of leadership as they

embrace and deploy the strategic-tactical-operational leadership paradigm outlined in chapter 2. Thus, as pastors read this book and become more willing to delegate, they will find time and opportunity to study church management principles more diligently and soon benefit more significantly from the synergies.

Chapter 10

1. Albert and Loy Morehead, eds. *The New American College Dictionary*, (New York: Signet, 1995).

2. Alistair Davidson, *Antonio Gramsci: Toward an Intellectual Biography* (London: Merlin Press, 1987). Antonio Gramsci was a political Marxist, and sought to propagate the theories of Marxism through *organic intellectuals* such as artists and writers. Despite his political leanings, his concept that societies need artists and leaders who can communicate important, grand concepts in simple, clear language is an important lesson for the church.

3. A good book on team-building exercises churches can employ at retreats and similar events is Harrison Snow's *Indoor/Outdoor Team Building Games For Trainers: Powerful Activities from the World of Adventure-Based Team Building and Ropes Courses* (New York: McGraw-Hill, 1997).

4. Churches of fifty to two hundred attendees are what Gary McIntosh describes as "relational in orientation," (*One Size Doesn't Fit All: Bringing Out the Best in Any Size Church*, [Grand Rapids, Mich.: Revell, 1999], 17–19). Because of this connection, knowing how everyone fits together in the body is of significant importance to congregants. Churches as small as fifty attendees should display an organizational flowchart, since even at these smaller sizes, churches are organizationally elaborate enough that not everybody will comprehend the relationships. Much confusion and awkwardness can be dispelled by publicly displaying an organizational flowchart. In tandem, a denominational flowchart can assist the local congregant in understanding how their local church fits into the global ministry of the Church.

5. Bob Whitesel and Kent R. Hunter, *A House Divided: Bridging the Generation Gaps in Your Church* (Nashville: Abingdon, 2001), 184–186. Among the Builder Generation, a church's organizational structure ranked fourth of the top five questions of newcomers. With boomers it ranked third, and with Generation X questions regarding the organizational structure of the church

ranked second. Thus, be aware that the younger the audience the more necessary it will be to explain the church's organizational and governmental configuration.

6. For a list of the varying types of small groups (sometimes called "cell" groups), along with a chart to see if you have enough small groups in each category, see "Four Steps to Celling a Church" in *Growth by Accident, Death by Planning: How Not to Kill a Growing Congregation* (Nashville: Abingdon, 2004), 139–148.

7. Acts 2:42–46 depicts four types of church growth. Numerical growth is usually incorrectly overemphasized when gauging progress toward church change. Thus, an analysis of *all four* types of biblical church growth is important for assessing the growth of a congregation during the change process. Here is a short overview of the four types of biblical church growth along with a concise suggestion for assessment.

FOUR TYPES OF CHURCH GROWTH

Growth in Maturity

Acts 2:42–43: "They devoted themselves to the apostles' teaching and to the fellowship, to the breaking of bread and to prayer. Everyone was filled with awe, and many wonders and miraculous signs were done by the apostles."

Assessment Suggestion. Compute the percentage of adults involved in biblical learning opportunities, such as regular Bible studies, Sunday schools, and home groups. If this percentage increases, for example if 35 percent were involved in learning groups in 2008 and 47 percent in 2009, then church growth in maturity may have occurred. While it is challenging to gauge progress in spiritual maturity, computing this percentage may be a general indicator of progress or regress. Thus, while a pastor may have not grown a church numerically, if he or she has fostered a percentage increase in growth in maturity, a type of church growth has resulted.

Growth in Unity

Acts 2:44–46: "All the believers were together and had everything in common. Selling their possessions and goods, they gave to anyone as he had need. Every day they continued to meet together in the temple courts. They broke bread in their homes and ate together with glad and sincere hearts."

Assessment Suggestion. A congregational poll can be helpful if it asks congregants to share how clearly they understand the church's vision. This exercise can assist in gauging the extent to which the congregation is united in purpose and goals.

Growth in Favor

Acts 2:47a: "Praising God and enjoying the favor of all the people."

Assessment Suggestion. Assessing growth in favor will require regular interaction with community residents. Personal conversations, as well as phone or Internet canvassing can help gauge public feelings toward a congregation. If the same polling process is conducted yearly, trends of growth in favor can be estimated.

Growth in Number

Acts 2:47b: "And the Lord added to their number daily those who were being saved."

Assessment Suggestion. Computing Average Annual Growth Rates (AAGRs) can be helpful for comparing numerical growth across years while compensating for the tendency of small numbers to distort the data. For a formula for computing your AAGR, see Elmer Towns, *Evangelism and Church Growth* (Ventura, Calif.: Regal Books, 1995), 23.

In the multifaceted church growth depicted in Acts 2:42–47, God is the one who contributed numbers. Thus it would seem the primary responsibilities of church leaders should be to foster the first three kinds of growth (maturity, unity, and community favor). It has been my experience that if church leaders foster the first three types of growth, the fourth will follow.